Snakes of Arabia

A Field Guide to the Snakes of the Arabian Peninsula and its Shores

Published with the support of
Domingo Garcia Llano

In collaboration with
Environment and Protected Areas Authority

Published by Motivate Publishing

Dubai: PO Box 2331, Dubai, UAE
Tel: (+971 4) 282 4060, fax: (+971 4) 282 0428
e-mail: books@motivate.ae   www.booksarabia.com

Dubai Media City: Office 508, Building No 8, Dubai Media City, Dubai, UAE
Tel: (+971 4) 390 3550, fax: (+971 4) 390 4845

Abu Dhabi: PO Box 43072, Abu Dhabi, UAE
Tel: (+971 2) 677 2005, fax: (+971 2) 677 0124

London: Acre House, 11/15 William Road, London NW1 3ER
e-mail: motivateuk@motivate.ae

Directors: Obaid Humaid Al Tayer and Ian Fairservice

Researched and written by Damien Egan

Consultant Editor: David Steele
Deputy Editor: Moushumi Nandy
Assistant Editor: Zelda Pinto
Art Director: Andrea Willmore
Designer: Cithadel Francisco

General Manager Books: Jonathan Griffiths
Publishing Coordinator: Jenny Bateman-Irish

Front cover: An Arabian Horned Viper
Back cover: A Sindh Saw-scaled Viper
Half-title page: An Afro-Asian Sand Snake

First published 2007

ISBN: 978 1 86063 239 6

British Library Cataloguing-in-Publication Data. A catalogue record for this book
is available from the British Library.

Printed and bound by International Printing Press, Dubai, UAE

Contents

Acknowledgements

There are many people I would like to thank for their assistance and support in the production of this book and it is quite impossible to prioritize anyone.

For their strong support and initial advice on the project, I'd like to thank Mr Abdulaziz Al Midfa, Director General of the EPAA, and Mr Christian Gross, the Director of Animal Management Consultancy, and the former Director of the Breeding Centre for Endangered Arabian Wildlife.

For their assistance in providing photographic and other material I thank Bill Branch, Wulf Haacke, Harold Voris, Zuhair Amr, Nashat Hamidan, Fareed Krupp, Wolfgang Wüster, Paul Vercammen, Peter Phelan, Jonathan Ali Khan, David Hegner, David Modrý, Drew Gardner, Tanya Sadler and James A Pointdexter II (USGS).

For assisting with the publishing process, and patiently advising on matters relating to software and computing, my thanks go to Kevin Budd.

For proofreading text and commenting on illustrations and other aspects of the book, I thank my colleagues at the Breeding Centre for Endangered Arabian Wildlife: Jane Edmonds; Kevin Budd; Andries Lottering; Paul Vercammen; Tanya Sadler and Peter Phelan.

I'd also like to thank Jane Edmonds and Vince Egan for reviewing the content and making suitable amendments.

For their invaluable assistance in the Reptile Department, I thank Mohammed Ishaq Basheer and Amara Suwa Arach'ge Don Dilan Sajeewa.

On a more personal note, I thank Tanya Sadler for her support and tolerance of my antisocial career path; Vincent and Lorraine Egan (my siblings) for "creating the monster" and years of valuable childhood learning; Margaret Egan, my mother, a default reptile person who can force-feed egg-eating snakes as well as the best and the Reed family for their kind hospitality and tolerance of yet another snake nerd (and his pets) in the years gone by.

My sincerest thanks go to Dave Morgan and Donald Strydom for their encouragement and support early in my herpetological career. Without their guidance I would never have progressed in the field.

Finally, and most importantly, my special thanks to Mr Domingo Garcia Llano whose financial support made this book possible. A falcon man by profession, Domingo has been a keen advocate of conservation of all manner of wildlife for many years. His enthusiasm and interest in all fauna, no matter how obscure, has been a tremendous encouragement to all of us at the Breeding Centre.

Author's Note

This book has taken me the better part of five years to complete. The main reason I undertook the project is because nothing really exists on the bookshelves in Arabia that is of much use. I receive countless calls, emails and letters with queries regarding snakebite, identifying snakes and what dangers (snake wise) one might expect when visiting the region. Many of those queries end in "Where can I get a decent book ?" Hopefully I've provided something useful to fill this gap.

The area covered in this book is peninsular Arabia – Saudi Arabia, Oman, United Arab Emirates, Yemen, Qatar and Bahrain. Although the Socotra islands are a part of Yemen, they are biogeographically distinct from mainland Arabia and have not been included.

The information in this book is as up-to-date as I can make it at present. Taxonomers are turning to DNA sequencing to properly determine the identity and origin of snakes. This means that there will probably be many name changes in the years to come. I have kept the names of snakes consistent with the majority of current literature, and acknowledge that there is not a complete consensus regarding many species. It is not my place to argue these points, but rather to inform the reader about the snakes themselves.

Although reptile husbandry is a large part of my job, I have purposely omitted any advice on keeping Arabian snakes in captivity. If such information was supplied in a bird field guide, there would be an outcry, and I feel the same way about reptiles. There is no reason why we can't passively observe these fascinating animals without bothering them.

A Note on Illustrations

The hand-drawn illustrations shown under the Species Identification Section were drawn from several sources. Where possible, I have drawn the pictures from live or preserved specimens. In the case of preserved specimens, I have used colour photographs to get a better reference of colour, sheen and so on. In some cases, it was simply impossible to use specimens, so in these pictures, coloured photos have been used as reference. These were cross-referenced against line drawings in scientific journals in order to get an accurate portrayal of the snake.

One species, the Aden black-headed snake, was not available as a specimen, photo or drawing, so I drew the snake using John Gasperetti's description (Gasperetti, 1988), referenced against the snake's closest Arabian relative, the Palestine black-headed snake. In this instance please allow for a little artistic licence.

The small, full-bodied drawings are there to point out the basic shape of the snake and the more common colour varieties that you may find them in. They are proportionate, but with no anatomical detail. What I've tried to achieve with these pictures, is to capture the "jizz" (to steal a bit of bird-watcher's slang) of the snake. In other words, the look of it at a first glance, or the features whereby the snake can be identified the quickest.

Introduction

Above: *A house snake.*

Following page: *An Afro-Asian sand snake.*

This book has been written to occupy an unfulfilled niche on the Arabian Peninsula. Although there are some excellent publications on various aspects of Arabian herpetology, this is the first in a field-guide format. There is little information in this book that is unknown to science, but a fair amount that is completely unknown to those who have no access to scientific journals. Snakes represent an ecological, and in some cases, medically significant factor throughout Arabia. Despite this there is little material available to assist people easily and accurately to identify snakes and diagnose treatment.

Within *Snakes of Arabia*, a balance has hopefully been struck by providing practical information for those wishing only to identify snakes, as well as facts on behaviour and natural history for people with a more specific interest in Arabian snakes. It is not a comprehensive reference volume, but a field aid to assist in correctly identifying snakes one might encounter. The selected references, listed at the end of the book gives a good cross reference of available material for those with a deeper academic interest in Arabian herpetofauna.

Snakes of Arabia is aimed at a wide variety of people and is, in the author's opinion, a sorely needed item in many fields of occupation. Doctors, teachers, naturalists, farmers, tour operators and just about anyone who is active outdoors should be able to make good use of it.

Despite the fact that some of the more common species are also highly venomous, snakebite in Arabia occurs less frequently than many might expect. It is, however, often the case that inappropriate treatment is administered in the event of a snakebite. There is little public education on the subject throughout the region. Hospital staff and medical practitioners are often ill-informed and ill-equipped to deal with such cases. The simple task of identifying the snake responsible for the bite can often become a complicated procedure.

In the snakebite section, symptoms and basic first aid protocols are explained and clearly illustrated. This section is primarily to guide the victim or helper in the right direction and warns of dangers inherent in commonly made mistakes. It has been drawn from tried and tested techniques but is not a medical text and should not be treated as such. Ultimately, the patient, having been treated with the correct first aid, should then rely on a medical professional to know the appropriate post-admission life-support protocol and suitable treatment.

Snake Distribution in Arabia

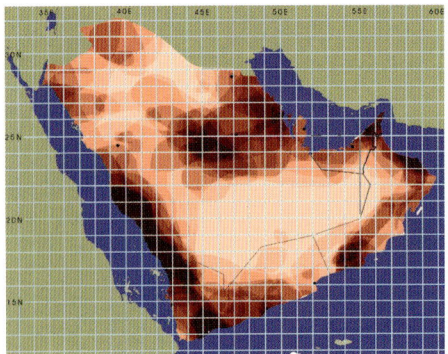

Fig 1. A collective overlay of all known snake distributions on the Arabian Peninsula.

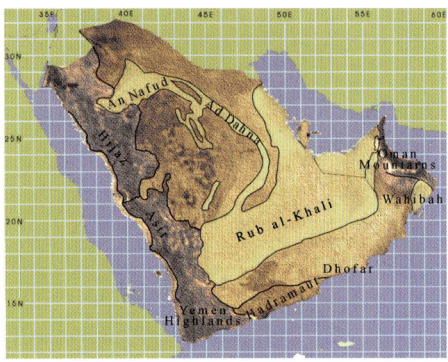

Fig 2. The major geographical features of the Arabian Peninsula.

As with virtually all fauna, Arabian snakes are distributed according to, among other things, local geography. Factors such as precipitation, temperature, vegetation and altitude influence the diversity and density of snake populations. The fauna of some regions in the Arabian Peninsula has been very well studied and documented, whereas other regions remain a mystery to science. Much of Yemen and specifically the Hadramaut Range has been subjected to very little collecting. There is every possibility that new species, as well as new information on the distribution of known species, could be discovered in years to come. This applies in many parts of the Arabian Peninsula and new localities, for various species are documented all the time.

Fig 1 shows a simplified representation of snake species diversity on the Arabian Peninsula. This is not strictly accurate, but simply a collective overlay of all known snake distributions. When this diagram is viewed alongside Fig 2, it becomes quite clear which geographical features give rise to the snake "hotspots" in the peninsula.

Several unique habitats can be found within the Arabian Peninsula, from vast sand deserts to canopy forest. It is easier to see why certain species are restricted to small areas, and why others are widespread, when one understands more about the lay of the land.

In this book, the Arabian Peninsula has been divided into six major geographical features. These are features that influence such factors as weather and faunal distribution on a peninsular level. Within these features are several types of habitat, which are also mentioned. The many smaller habitats and many more microhabitats that exist are innumerable and are only mentioned where they have a direct influence on the distribution of a species.

A Sindh saw-scaled viper on a rocky outcrop.

Western Mountain Complex

HIJAZ RANGE

This feature runs parallel to the Red Sea Coast from the Dead Sea in the north, southwards to the vicinity of 21ºN. It is separated from the sea by a wide, sandy coastal plain. This area is arid and receives no regular rain, but rather occasional sporadic downpours. Much of the region might go without any precipitation for more than a year with most areas receiving less than 50 mm per year. Precipitation is highest at higher elevations.

The mountains here are rugged and sparsely vegetated with little surface water. Steep-sided wadis and jagged, seemingly barren mountains characterize the landscape.

To the east, the mountains fragment as they enter the interior. Here sedimentary outcrops are interspersed with stony plains and volcanic remnants. These eventually meet the An Nafud Sands in the Northern Interior, or a mountain/stony plain mosaic in the Central Interior.

Geography of Arabia

ASIR RANGE, YEMEN HIGHLANDS AND TIHAMA

This is simply the southern continuation of the Hijaz. The characteristic landscape that defines the Asir starts near Taif and extends to south-western Yemen, ending before the western Hadramaut Mountains. Exposure to annual monsoons results in the area being relatively wetter than the Hijaz complex. This is more so in the southern highlands which lie in a more direct path of the monsoon rains. Rainfall of over 1,000 mm per year has been recorded in the high-lying areas. A wide coastal plain, Tihama, fringes the Red Sea and the Gulf of Aden, and receives the benefits of runoff. This littoral is heavily cultivated as are many of the fertile foothills, which have been terraced for agriculture. The landscape is characterized by high, steep mountains, well-vegetated valleys, woodland and arid savannah. Towards the interior the mountains give way to arid steppes with occasional outcrops and eventually the sand desert of Rub al-Khali in the north-east.

Above: Hijaz Mountains, Saudi Arabia.

Below: A plateau at an elevation of approximately 2,500 m above sea level near Sana'a, Yemen.

Above: A wadi in the Yemen highlands.

Below, left: Subsistence agriculture at the mountain foothills of northern Yemen.

Below, right: Riverine woodland typical of the south-western mountains of Asir.

Hadramaut Complex

This range forms a natural ecological barrier between the Yemen highlands and the Dhofar Mountains of Oman. In the west, the range forks into two ridges that extend in an easterly direction. These ridges form the north and south walls of the massive Wadi Hadramaut, an enormous drainage basin. Much of the land area of the north ridge is north facing, resulting in an arid, dry environment. Small patches of arid woodland and even grassland exist, but not as a continuous corridor. This ridge extends east, almost to Dhofar and excludes many of the species dependent on a wetter environment. The southern ridge receives peripheral monsoon rain and is relatively well vegetated with woodland in places. This ridge terminates at the mouth of Wadi Hadramaut near 51°E. The cliffs of the southern ridge enter the sea directly in some places, and are separated by coastal plain in others. North of the Hadramaut, the landscape becomes progressively more arid as it enters gravel plains and the sands of the Rub al-Khali.

Above: Wadi Hadramaut, seen from the northern ridge. The range to the left of the picture is the north-facing aspect of the southern ridge.

Left: Small patches of arid grassland and savannah exist near springs on the northern ridge.

Top: *Barren, stony plateau on the northern ridge of Wadi Hadramaut.*

Above: *Seen here is a tributary wadi with perennial water.*

Left: *A view of the northern Hadramaut showing the flat plateau, deeply incised by tributary wadis.*

Dhofar Complex

The Dhofar Mountains form the eastern end of the southern escarpment. South-facing slopes are directly in line of the monsoons, and are lush with dense woodland and canopy forest in areas. Foothills and coastal plains consist of grassland and scrub. In some areas the mountains terminate into the sea, and in others wide coastal plains separate them from the sea.

During the monsoon, wide streams, waterfalls, rain and mist characterize the landscape. At other times of the year the landscape is browner in appearance, but still rich in perennial vegetation. The north-facing slopes are more arid. North of the escarpment lies a stony desert with sedimentary outcrops and extensive plains, which end further northwards in the sands of the Rub al-Khali, and extend north-east to the Oman Mountains.

Above: *Wadi Darbat in Salalah, during the height of the monsoon season.*

Left: *A temporary lake formed by monsoon rains at Al Mughsayl in Dhofar.*

Above: *Jebel Qara, Dhofar, during the dry season. Note that perennial vegetation is still rich in the region.*

Left: *Stony desert with sedimentary outcrops just north of the Dhofar Escarpment.*

Below: *The edge of the Rub al-Khali, near the border between UAE and Saudi Arabia.*

Rub al-Khali Sand Desert Complex (The Empty Quarter)

This area consists of about 600,000 sq km of uninterrupted sandy desert in the southern interior of the Arabian Peninsula. Vegetation is absent from much of the region and is sparse where present. The area receives little rain, and may go for years without significant rain. Naturally the climatic extremes of such an environment have a marked effect on local fauna, and the only snake species to venture any distance into the Rub al-Khali are horned vipers and Arabian sand boas. Giant wind-blown sand dunes characterize the landscape of the Empty Quarter. The peripheral areas include gravel plains as well as salty *sabkha* marshes.

Top: *An aerial view of the central region of the Rub al-Khali, Saudi Arabia.*

Above: *Stands of* ghaf *trees near the edge of Rub al-Khali.*

Right: *Near the UAE-Saudi Arabia border.*

Eastern Mountain Complex

This complex consists of a chain of territories collectively known as the Oman Mountains. They start as the Musandam Peninsula in the north and end near Ra's al-Hadd in the south. The northern part of this range (Musandam and eastern UAE) consists of arid mountains with sparse vegetation and steep, gravel and boulder-strewn wadis. There is little surface water, but wadis containing perennial streams are often well vegetated and fauna rich. The higher Musandam is relatively wetter than the Al Hajar Mountains of the UAE. The mountains either end in the sea, or are separated from the sea by coastal plains and beaches. Towards the south, the coastal plains widen considerably and local precipitation increases. Fringing the Oman Mountains on the arid western side, are several large gravel plains often with sparse acacia woodland. Further west, the mountains fragment or end abruptly in sandy desert. To the south, the Wahiba Desert marks the end of the Oman Mountains. To the south-east, the massive gravel plains of the Jiddat al-Harasis plateau extend all the way to Dhofar.

Above: *The Musandam Mountains at 1,100 m above sea level (between Dibba and Khasab, Oman).*

Left: *The Al Hajar Mountains with foothills and coastal plains in the background (near Fujairah, UAE).*

17

Top: *Perennial pools in Wadi Shawkah in the UAE.*

Above, left: *Acacia woodland west of the Oman Mountains (near Masafi, UAE).*

Above, right: *A dry wadi bed in Wadi Al Bih, Oman.*

Northern Interior

This area lies between the western mountain complex and the east coast of Saudi Arabia, south to the Rub al-Khali. It contains two major sandy deserts: the An Nafud Sands in the north-west, and a long corridor of sand known as Ad Dahna. The latter forms a bow shape as it curves from a south-easterly direction to south, just east of Riyadh and joins with the Rub al-Khali at around 21ºN. West of Ad Dahna and roughly parallel to it, lies the mountain escarpment of Jebel Tuwaiq. Alluvial fans characterize the eastern slopes of this range. Alluvial plains, interspersed with sparsely vegetated sandy desert and flat gravel plains extend to the shores of the Arabian Gulf. Oases and drainage systems are key features of the north-eastern peninsula.

Marine Environment

The seas surrounding the Arabian Peninsula consist of the Gulf of Oman, the Arabian Gulf, the Gulf of Aden and the Red Sea. Ocean floor topography is the strongest influencing factor affecting sea snake populations. The Arabian Gulf is generally less than 80 m deep and consists of warm sheltered water, ideal for several species occupying it. The part of the Gulf of Oman fringing northern Oman and eastern UAE gets progressively deeper further south. The southern coastline has an abrupt drop off to waters exceeding 1,000 m, thus forming a barrier for snakes, preventing them from colonizing the Red Sea. The Red Sea itself consists of waters in excess of 2,500 m in the central rift, but has wide, shallow shelves along most of the Arabian shoreline.

Top: Turbid water with a sandy substrate (Ajman, UAE).

Above: A reef containing hard corals, sponges and macroalgae (Muscat, Oman).

Left: A shrimp goby, possibly more of an attraction for sea snakes than their actual habitat.

Above: *A wadi racer evades the attention of a school of banded terapons in an estuary in Dhofar.*

Below: *A juvenile cat snake.*

General Adaptations of Snakes to their Environment

Snakes have occupied almost every ecological niche on the Arabian Peninsula. As some of these environments are among the harshest on earth, certain snakes have evolved some extreme adaptations in order to survive. Some have evolved to the point that they are completely dependent on their chosen environment and have become specialized desert dwellers. Others can tolerate extremes, but are generalists that can thrive in most Arabian biotopes. Others, not so adaptable, are restricted to patches of milder habitat.

All snakes have certain features in common that aid in basic survival. The most effective of these, and one that is applicable in any environment, is a very economical metabolism. Snakes, like all reptiles, are ectotherms. This means that they cannot internally regulate their own body temperature but rely on an external source, the sun, for warmth. A stationary reptile therefore expends very little energy whereas a stationary mammal or

A Sindh saw-scaled viper covered in water droplets.

bird uses a great deal more. The advantage of this for the snake is the fact that it can go for several weeks or even months without food or water as long as it remains relatively inactive. This adaptation has allowed certain snakes to colonize deserts and other extreme environments, as well as being successful in areas with high levels of competition for food by other species.

Snakes have several other adaptations to aid in conserving fluids and energy. The skin, devoid of pores, is virtually impermeable which means that very little moisture is lost through it. Urination takes place in a chalky, or gel-like mass, rather like that of most birds. This ensures that very little water is excreted as waste and therefore relatively little water needs to be consumed in the first place. Most snakes will drink when surface water is available, but many will go through life without physically drinking at all, meeting their moisture requirements by utilizing the liquid in the bodies of prey animals.

Others utilize dew or condensed coastal fog that settles early morning.

Specific Adaptations

Apart from the general characteristics shared by all snakes, many of the niche-specific species have very interesting adaptations that allow them to occupy their own part of the peninsula.

Species adapted for sandy deserts are usually smaller in size and feed on reptiles and occasionally desert rodents. Three species of viper and one species of sand boa also eat soft-bodied invertebrates.

Physical adaptations and behavioural patterns are varied, and allow each species to fill a smaller niche within the greater desert environment.

Two species, the Arabian sand boa, and the Arabian horned viper, are probably more specifically adapted for harsh desert survival than any other.

Sand boas are smooth-scaled snakes with plough-shaped snouts and small eyes. These features enable easy manoeuvrebility as they shuffle through loose sand, well under the surface. Sand boas are able to occupy the most barren deserts, as they do not rely on rodent burrows or vegetation for shelter.

Horned vipers are also specifically adapted for desert life, but in dramatically different ways. They have roughly keeled scales that form small ridges down the back and sides of the snake that trap sand as the snake shuffles its body just under the surface. This aids to camouflage

the snake when ambushing prey or otherwise concealing itself. The rough scales, when rubbed against one another, are used as an audible warning, should the snake be harassed. The same adaptations can be observed in the saw-scaled vipers and a few non-venomous species. Hissing often involves opening the mouth and exposing the moist interior to evaporation. Horned vipers are dependent on vegetation or pre-existing burrows to use as shelters during the hot daytime hours and are thus absent from much of the central regions of the Empty Quarter.

Most snakes in Arabia are generalists. There are some, such as the hooded Malpolon, Afro-Asian sand snake and the Sindh saw-scaled viper that thrive in true desert, but can make themselves comfortable in a wide range of habitats as well. Sand snakes and saw-scaled vipers seem to have adapted to another extreme and have successfully colonized roadside greenbelts, suburban gardens and rural human settlements, undoubtedly attracted by the large numbers of sparrows and other birds that nest in these situations, as well as a ready supply of house geckos and rodents.

Many Arabian species are completely unsuited to desert life, but are not necessarily habitat specific either. Most of these species live in the southern and western mountains where monsoon rainfall allows for a less barren

Above: An Arabian horned viper partially buried in sand.

Below: The Afro-Asian sand snake is a true generalist, thriving in most environments.

The Sindh saw-scaled viper is an accomplished desert survivor, but is commonly found in gardens and plantations.

environment. Most Arabian species with an East African affinity, such as puff adders and cobras, fall into this group as do a few small Palaearctic species (racers etc).

Many snakes have distributions limited to particular altitudes. An extreme example of this is the Persian horned viper, which (in Arabia), only seems to occupy the Oman Mountains at altitudes of over 600 m above sea level. It is unclear why they do not occur in the mountain valleys, as their current habitat is bleak with a very sparse prey-base. Presumably they are out-competed by the more common Oman carpet vipers that occupy the wadis. This type of competition probably has a marked effect on snake populations within other species in Arabia.

The final frontier of snake occupation, the sea, demands complete adaptation to survive. The Arabian Gulf and Arabian Sea have nine or more species of sea snakes. Interestingly, no species of sea snakes occur in the Red Sea. As sea snakes favour shallow, sheltered water, the steep drop-off of most of the southern Arabian coastline (southern Oman and Yemen) to depths of more than 1,000 m excludes sea snakes and prevents them from going further west. The pelagic sea snake, although not dependent on shallow water, is also absent from the Red Sea, but has been found in the Gulf of Aden. The factors influencing this species' Arabian distribution are largely unknown.

Every part of a sea snake's body is specifically adapted to the marine environment. Although all sea snakes need to breathe air at the surface, an enlarged air sack allows them to remain submerged and active for several hours at a time! The nostrils are shaped into watertight valves. All sea snakes have a laterally compressed tail as well as at least the last-third of the body to assist propulsion. One species, the pelagic

Arabian Snakes: An Overview

sea snake is compressed from head to tail. Most sea snakes have difficulty crawling, or even righting themselves on land and often perish if stranded on the beach. Many species have roughly keeled scales and the males of certain species, most notably the short sea snake, have well-developed sharp spines along the flanks. The reasons for such protrusions are unclear, but it may be assumed that these spinose scales might assist in purchase during mating. Rough scales in general may help sea snakes anchor themselves to rock or coral in strong currents.

The most unusual adaptations among the sea snakes must be those of the small-headed sea snake. The deep body looks completely out of proportion to the tiny head and long neck region. This however, is a perfect adaptation to catching small eels and gobies, down holes.

Above, left: *An annulated sea snake taking air. All sea snakes need to breathe at the surface.*

Above, right: *A small-headed sea snake. There's no mistaking this unusual species.*

Below: *An Arabian Gulf sea snake.*

Venomous Snakes

It is easy to understand why certain species of snakes on the Arabian Peninsula are highly venomous. In an environment where every ounce of energy wasted is a step closer to possible death, the ability to simply stab a pair of fangs into a prey animal to subdue it is a great advantage.

The primary function of snake venom is to kill or subdue prey in order to eat it. Due to the fact that many venom types are rich in digestive enzymes, a secondary function in some species is as a digestive agent, effectively beginning the digestive process before the prey item is even swallowed.

Certain snakes use venom as a direct means of defence. This is not common though and usually involves exceptional circumstances. Most predatory animals will bite in defence if they have no choice and a snake is no exception. The primary defence is evasion. Biting is always a last resort. It should also be noted that many bites are 'dry bites' - the snake does not inject venom when biting.

In Arabia, most bites are by slow moving, ground dwelling species such as vipers. These snakes, however, tend to be tolerant of passive thoroughfare and only generally strike if provoked or restrained. Most are

Above: An Oman carpet viper. A common and irascible venomous snake from the eastern mountains.

Left: An Arabian horned viper eating a cheeseman's gerbil. The primary function of snake venom is to kill prey.

Arabian Snakes: An Overview

well camouflaged and rely on this to remain unnoticed. If harassed, they all have effective visual and audible warnings, not necessarily to threaten, but often to attract attention to the fact that they are around. This would help if an ungulate or other animal were about to accidentally tread on the snake.

Most snakes will bite if restrained or subjected to prolonged antagonism. Most of the slower venomous snakes have a quick acting component in the venom (cytotoxin) that will cause an immediate burning pain. Puff adders have a cytotoxin as a primary component in the venom. Most of the smaller desert vipers have a cytotoxic element along with a more potent haemotoxin. In most cases where the snake was not noticed prior to the bite, the snake was trodden upon or a hand was placed on it by accident. A snake should not be blamed for human negligence such as unobservant behaviour or failure to wear protective clothing.

DANGEROUS SNAKES IN ARABIA

There is a distinct difference between the most dangerous snakes in Arabia and the most venomous. The most accurate way of determining which species is the most dangerous is by looking at snakebite statistics, which are unfortunately largely inaccurate and incomplete for most of the region.

The most venomous land snake in Arabia is possibly the Arabian cobra. In nature, however, it uses its speed and agility to escape, usually even before being detected and are therefore responsible for few bites. It is normally the slow moving species, or ones that are willing to live close to human activity that end up adding to the snakebite statistics.

In the western and southern mountain complexes, the Burton's carpet viper is responsible for the highest percentage of snakebite. Burrowing asps would also be accountable for a certain percentage each

Above: *Arabian horned vipers tend to be tolerant of passive thoroughfare.*

Below: *Burrowing asps are greatly feared throughout much of their range. Their preference for loose soil make them a potential danger for agricultural workers.*

year. These snakes favour agricultural land where labourers and farm workers are at risk.

The Oman carpet viper is responsible for higher numbers of snakebite than others along much of the eastern coastal fringe. Many wadis in the Oman Mountains have become popular recreational areas in recent years increasing the potential for human exposure to carpet vipers. In the eastern deserts of Arabia, the Sindh saw-scaled viper is both common and highly venomous and could represent a potential hazard. It is unclear what the rate of snakebite is in eastern Arabia, but the author has personally only ever heard of one confirmed saw-scaled viper bite. The snake has, however been the confirmed culprit of livestock bites on many occasions. The Arabian horned viper is common throughout the

region, but has comparatively mild venom and fatalities would be very much the exception. Sea snakes, despite possessing some of the most potent toxins of all snakes, are relatively harmless unless directly tampered with. It is surprising, but a good reflection on the snakes' temperament, that bites do not occur regularly in the gulf. Not only is there a great amount of fishing activity in the area, in which hundreds of sea snakes are taken as by-catch, but also a fair number of live juvenile sea snakes stranded on the beaches (including public bathing beaches) after storm and wind conditions. There are nine species of sea snakes in the Arabian waters, including fairly aggressive species such as the beaked sea snake, yet records of bites are practically non-existent in the region.

Venom

Venom is essentially a modified form of saliva. It is generally composed of a number of enzymes, causing different effects on the body. Venom could probably be classified into hundreds of types, but for all practical applications, in terms of the effect on the body, it can be split into three or four types.

Snake venom differs from species to species, as well as widely distributed members of the same species in some cases. It has evolved according to that snake's specific habits, habitat and prey base.

Cytotoxin (Cell-affecting Venom)

As the name implies, cytotoxins are cell destroying. A bite from a cytotoxic snake generally produces local pain and swelling around the bite site. In severe bites, and those of the larger cytotoxic snakes this can spread to the rest of the limb. Depending on the exact nature of the venom, discolouring and necrosis can also result. Most people bitten by cytotoxic snakes survive only with a painful lesson as a reminder, but in some cases, most notably the puff adder in Arabia, disfigurement may occur. Large-scale necrosis, or even gangrene can result in digits or limbs being amputated. Massive tissue damage can also cause irreparable damage to nerves and

muscles, causing various levels of disability. In Arabia puff adders have predominantly cytotoxic venom. Carpet vipers, saw-scaled vipers, horned vipers and false horned vipers all have a cytotoxic element in their venom in conjunction with another, generally more potent venom. Although fatalities are known, and do occur as a result of cytotoxic bites, they are more often than not caused by secondary infections (often the result of poor snakebite management). Other less common causes of death from cytotoxic bites are either through being bitten into an artery, vein or other area of high circulation, or succumbing to an allergic reaction (anaphylaxis).

Above: *The puff adder produces a cytotoxin, causing massive tissue damage locally.*

Below: *Most small vipers, such as this Oman carpet viper, have a haemotoxic venom.*

Haemotoxin (Blood-affecting Venom)

Haemotoxic venom affects the clotting process of the blood. This type of venom is more life threatening than cytotoxins because it affects the body systemically. It is, however, quite slow to act on the body and may take several hours, or even days to start presenting. Symptoms of a bite would include haemorrhaging (bleeding) possibly from the bite wound, but more commonly internally. Areas of discoloured skin, the passing of blood in urine, bleeding gums, bloodshot eyes and headaches are all possible signs of internal bleeding. Death would result from massive internal heamorrhaging or renal (kidney) failure.

Local pain and swelling often accompany other symptoms. This however, may well be a sign of a cytotoxin present in the venom.

Arabian species that possess a haemotoxin as a primary venom are saw-scaled vipers of the genus *Echis* and horned vipers.

Neurotoxin (Nerve-affecting Venom)

Bites from neurotoxic snakes (desert black snake, Arabian cobra, false horned viper) should be treated promptly. This is fast acting venom and is potentially life threatening.

Neurotoxins affect the central nervous system, causing the major organs or muscles controlled by those nerves to malfunction. A bite may result in a tingling and mildly painful sensation starting at the bite site, and spreading away. The eyelids become heavy and the pupils often dilate. Facial muscles become partially paralyzed; breathing is laboured, and the patient may find it difficult to swallow. Often the patient appears rather drunk and incoherent, and is unable to balance or speak properly. The most common cause of death in neurotoxic bites is asphyxiation due to paralysis of the diaphragm muscle, or heart failure.

Above: *Arabian cobra. Bites from snakes with neurotoxic venom should be treated promptly.*

Below: *A yellow sea snake. Sea snake venom is classified as neurotoxic by some authors and myotoxic by others.*

Myotoxin (Muscle-affecting Venom)

This venom affects the smooth, or involuntary muscles in the body, rendering them paralyzed. Symptoms include physical fatigue, drooping eyelids and laboured breathing and mildly painful, or sensitive muscles, as well as paralysis of the muscles. The venom of most sea snakes is classified as myotoxic by most authors and neurotoxic by others. Symptoms certainly differ from most terrestrial neurotoxic snakes, but such differences are naturally to be expected, given sea snakes' lifestyles and choice of prey. There are few documented bites from many of the species, so consistent information regarding symptoms is rare.

Snakebite

Treating snakebite, in terms of first aid, can be performed by anyone with minimal equipment and experience. Most of us will go through life never even meeting anyone that has been bitten by a snake, but should the situation occur where one is bitten, or is required to give assistance to a snakebite patient, it is imperative that there is a clear plan of action. A large part of treating snakebite is psychological. It is easy to panic and lose control. Remaining calm, whether patient or practitioner, will be of great advantage and go a long way.

In many instances incorrect treatment of snakebite has actually caused more damage than the original bite! As important as it is to know what to do, it is probably even more important to know what must never be done.

Do Not!

DO NOT PANIC!

This is often easier said than done, but it is vital to keep your composure and maintain a steady frame of mind. Whether you have been bitten, or treating someone who has, losing your head will serve nobody. The more calm the victim, the slower the body's fluids are moving. This allows for more time prior to hospitalization and treatment.

DO NOT USE A TOURNIQUET!

This is a commonly used first aid procedure for snakebite. It will cut off the blood supply, and concentrate the venom in one small area without restricting its movement within that area. In the case of a bite from a cytotoxic snake, this technique will amplify local symptoms. Tourniquets left in place for extended periods can result in infections such as gangrene. Digit and even limb loss have been the result of this type of treatment.

DO NOT CUT OPEN, OR SUCK THE WOUND!

This is going to open the wound up to possible infection, and the amount of venom one might remove in this manner will be negligible in comparison to the damage caused. The venom is absorbed into the lymph; a process best compared to liquid being dropped into a sponge. The liquid is passed from cell to cell, in all directions, and to try and suck all of that liquid back out of a small opening will not be an option without doing serious damage.

DO NOT RUB ANY MEDICATION INTO THE WOUND!

Potassium permanganate crystals were widely used in the past; these have proved to be ineffective in the treatment of snakebite. The less aggravation around the bite site, the better.

DO NOT TAKE ANY PAINKILLERS, DRUGS OR ALCHOHOL!

These may interfere with your metabolism and heart rate. Side effects of even over-the-counter painkillers can create symptoms that may hamper an accurate diagnosis. Although being calm is important, it is also important for the patient to be completely coherent and aware of what is happening.

DO NOT EXERT YOURSELF OR THE PATIENT MORE THAN NEEDED!

Running is going to increase the heart rate, which, in turn will allow the venom in the body to spread to vital organs at a faster rate. If the bite victim is a long way from help, then walking for 10 minutes, and resting for five is a better option. If the victim can be transported directly by vehicle, then so much the better.

DO NOT TRY TO CATCH OR KILL THE SNAKE FOR IDENTIFICATION!

Snakes are often tricky to catch. Doing this is not only wasting time, but also often putting another person at risk of being bitten. Snakes are difficult to kill, and reflex actions can often cause the head to continue 'functioning' for several hours after it has been chopped off.

Many people have been 'bitten' by snakes whose heads have been severed. If the identification criteria used in this book are referred to, a description of the snake should be possible without further risk. If the snake has been killed however, and you are sure it is dead, then bring it along for identification. Store the dead snake in a hard, clear container to prevent further accidents.

TREAT ANTIVENOM WITH CAUTION!

Unless you have had prior training in antivenom use, it is advised that the antivenom accompany the patient to hospital, rather than be applied in the field. Many people are allergic to horse-based antivenom and the resulting anaphylactic shock could be far more immediately life-threatening than any venom.

Do!

APPLY IMMEDIATE PRESSURE

This can be done by pressing the heel of the palm over the area of the bite. Do not waste time with this if you are on your own, as you need a spare hand for bandaging.

APPLY PRESSURE BANDAGE

A 10 cm or wider, crepe bandage should be wrapped around the entire bitten limb. It is not too important which side you start from, just as long as it covers as wide an area as possible. Wrap the bandage with the same amount of pressure as if treating a sprained ankle or wrist.

Moving the joints of the bitten limb will speed up lymph flow, so a splint can be put in place to immobilize the area - this is optional. Use fingers or toes of the bitten limb as an indicator as to whether the bandage is too tight or not. Pinch to test for sensation, and check the colour. If the limb or digits swell up, turn blue, or lose sensation, the bandage should be removed and the whole procedure repeated. The best way of doing this is by simultaneously unwinding the first bandage and wrapping the new one in its place, so that pressure has not been completely removed from the limb prior to the application of the new bandage. If a bandage is not available, a shirt, or similar item can be torn into strips and used instead.

Snakebite

GET THE BITE VICTIM TO HOSPITAL AS SOON AS POSSIBLE

If possible, get an ambulance to come to you.

CARDIO-PULMONARY MASSAGE (CPR)

If the victim stops breathing, or experiences heart failure, then cardio-pulmonary massage as well as mouth-to-mouth resuscitation can be applied. Make sure you know what you are doing! Also know your local laws as to the liability should something go wrong. A basic first-aid course, offered by many institutions worldwide is highly recommended for anyone active in the outdoors.

REMEMBER

Remove all rings, bracelets and other tight fitting jewellery or clothing. These items can cause major constriction in the case of swelling.

If you have antivenom, take it along to the hospital with you. The more antivenom available, the more the doctor's options are.

Always try to keep a patient calm. Do not incite a feeling of panic with your own actions. Be as reassuring as possible.

TREATING A BITE TO THE HEAD OR TRUNK

Apply pressure over the bitten area. This can be done by rolling up a bandage, socks, shirt etc into a tight ball and placing it firmly over the bite site. A bandage can be used to strap the wad firmly in place. A similar technique is often employed in the case of gunshot wounds. These bites should be treated with haste as they are usually near areas of high circulation, as well as close to vital organs. Many such bites are caused when a sleeping person rolls over on a snake. Multiple bites are thus quite common and usually more severe.

ALLERGIC SHOCK

Some people are hypersensitive to snake venom, or antivenom. In these cases the victim may stop breathing within a few minutes and go into anaphylactic shock. Adrenaline is effective for treating anaphylaxis and can be administered via an injection into a large muscle (thigh or buttocks). Adrenaline (epinephrine) is available in self-injecting syringe kits. These are mostly marketed for bee-sting allergies. This is a convenient and easy-to-use form of administering adrenaline.

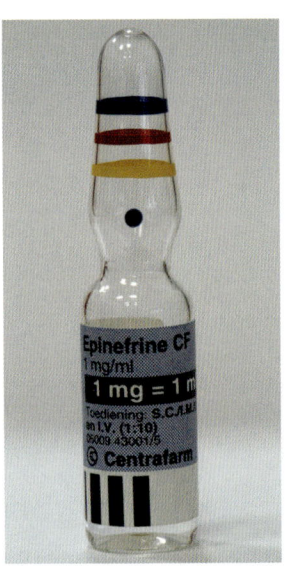

Adrenaline is normally marketed in glass vials.

Top, left: Apply immediate pressure.

Top, right: Apply pressure bandage from either side of the bitten limb.

Above: Ensure that the bandage is evenly wrapped around the entire limb.

Left: Apply a sling to help immobilize the limb.

nakebite

Antivenom Treatment

The vast majority of snakebite cases in Arabia will not necessarily require antivenom. If a layperson commits to using antivenom in the field, he should be completely aware of the potential side effects as well as the possibility that the patient is hypersensitive. It is due to these potential side-effects that antivenom should be treated with the utmost caution.

WHEN TO ADMINISTER ANTIVENOM

As a fist aid treatment, antivenom is only likely to be necessary in sea snakes, Arabian cobras and possibly desert black snakes and puff adders, although most bites from any of these can be treated without antivenom if the patient is hospitalized in good time.

Only obvious life-threatening symptoms warrant the use of antivenom in the field and the helper should be aware of shock, panic and other psychosomatic symptoms that may hamper diagnosis.

If the patient appears drunk, with hooded eyelids, dilated pupils and is experiencing difficulty in speaking and breathing, this would be indicative of systemic poisoning. This would probably be the only situation where antivenom need be administered by a layperson. In some extreme cases puff adder bites showing extreme swelling and systemic symptoms, may need antivenom, but most cases can wait until the patient is hopitalized.

It is very important to question the victim about his history of allergy. Ask if they have any allergies, or if they have a history of eczema, asthma or other conditions relating to allergies. These are indicators that the patient might experience an allergic reaction to antivenom treatment. Adrenaline should be on standby to counter such a reaction.

STORAGE AND USE OF ANTIVENOM

Antivenom is generally supplied in liquid form in 10 ml glass vials. It may be colourless or amber in appearance but is always clear. Cloudy antivenom should be discarded at once, as it is of no use. When not in use, antivenom should be stored in temperatures, between 2°C and 8°C. It should not be frozen as this could lead to the glass vial cracking. When used in the field, some kind of cooling arrangement should be made. A small cooler box packed with dry-ice bricks is ideal.

All antivenom is marked with an expiry date. This should be adhered to and new stock should be bought well prior to expiry. Recently expired antivenom can be used if no fresh material is available as long as the liquid is completely clear and has no cloudiness or sediment.

The amount of antivenom carried depends on local species and the budget limitations of the person involved. The more antivenom available after a bite, the more options the medical practitioner has. Some severe elapid, or large viper bites might require 20 or more ampoules.

What is Antivenom?

The process by which antivenom is made is similar to that of most vaccines.

Venom is extracted from snakes under laboratory conditions and is freeze-dried or otherwise preserved to retain its potency.

The venom is then injected into animals, usually horses but sometimes goats, in tiny quantities until that animal builds immunity against the effects of the venom. After some time the animal will build up a great resistance to the venom and will suffer no major effects even when normally lethal doses of venom are injected. At this stage the animal is known as hyperimmunized. Whole blood is then drawn, separated and refined. The resulting refined serum is bottled and stored as antivenom. Monovalent antivenoms are produced by exposing the animal to the venom of only one species of snake and is usually only effective against the bites of that species. Polyvalent antivenom covers a number of species.

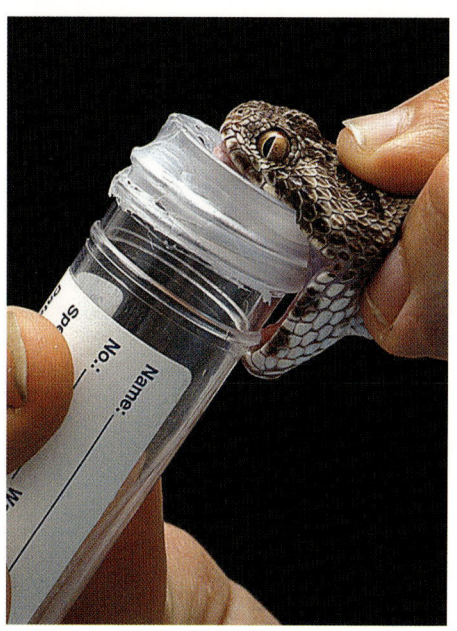

Outdoor First Aid Kit

A simple snakebite kit should be carried by anyone who is active outdoors. Most of the contents, with the exception of snakebite antivenom, is available at any pharmacy. Antivenom is generally available directly from the producers, and the cost is variable depending on the type.

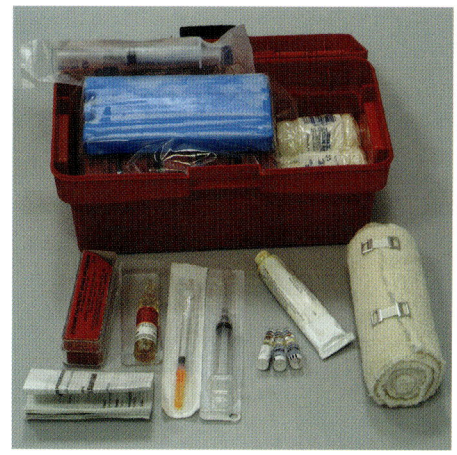

Above: *A saw-scaled viper during venom extraction. This is the first stage in the antivenom production.*

Right: *This is the author's first aid kit and includes: elasticated bandages; antivenom; plenty of spare syringes; adrenaline and an antihistamine ointment (for insect bites).*

This worm lizard resembles a small snake. Note the scales that are formed into rings. No snakes have this form of scale patterning.

Is it a Snake?

A few other reptiles, and even invertebrates, may resemble small snakes at a glance. Worm lizards have elongated bodies and no legs, and may closely resemble blind snakes or sand boas. Certain species of skink also have elongated bodies with reduced limbs. Most snakes have scale rows that run diagonally, like a fishing net, or chain-link fence, whereas skinks have transverse rows of scales, turning into even rows of broad, roughly square scales on the belly, like kitchen tiles. Worm lizards are easily identified by the rings of scales running around the body. Certain worms, slugs and leeches have a passing resemblance to small snakes in shape, but do not have scales, and are generally moist and slimy.

Field Identification

Catching or otherwise restraining a snake for identification is unwise and can be dangerous. Apart from this, it is unfair on the snake. It is sound practice to observe without disturbing unless you have very good reason to do otherwise. Some snakes are a bit confusing to identify and it is important to know exactly what to look for to make a correct identification. Most snakes can be observed and accurately identified at a short distance. There are very few snakes in Arabia that so closely resemble one another that very close scrutiny is needed. Following are a few criteria useful in identifying snakes in the field.

Fig 3. Typical body shapes of snakes.

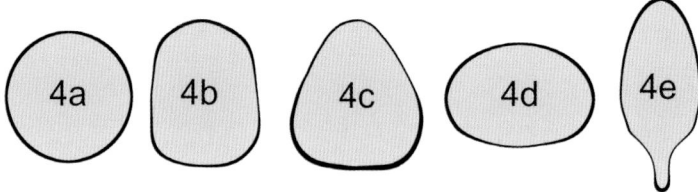

Fig 4. Typical shapes of snakes when viewed in cross section. 4a – round; 4b – laterally compressed; 4c – sub-triangular; 4d – flattened; 4e – compressed with keel (sea snakes).

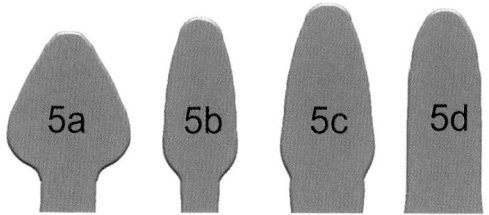

Fig 5. Typical head shapes of snakes. 5a – broad distinct head (vipers); 5b – moderate, distinct head (most typical snakes); 5c – moderate, slightly distinct head (most sea snakes, sand boas); 5d – indistinct head (worm snakes, burrowing asps).

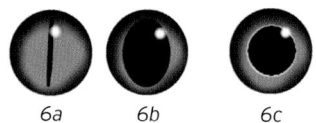

Fig 6. Typical pupil shapes of snakes.
6a – contracted elliptical pupil; 6b – dilated elliptical pupil; 6c – round pupil.

How to Identify Snakes

SHAPE AND FORM

The general shape of the body should be observed. Is it thin, medium or fat?

Check if the head is easily distinguishable from the body by a thinner neck area or not.

If possible the shape of the body as a cross section should be noted. Some snakes are flattened, some round and some laterally compressed. Any other outstanding features, such as horns, rough scales, shiny sheen, big head etc should naturally be noted. Eyes should be closely scrutinized if possible. Check the size and positioning and establish if the pupils are round or elliptical (cat-like).

LOCATION

Note the geographical location where the snake was found. If you do not have a GPS (global positioning system), estimation will suffice (eg: approximately 20 km west of Al Dhaid, UAE). This area can later be matched to a map to get information such as altitude.

Note also the habitat and position that the snake was found in (eg: sandy, vegetated desert, under a small bush on south-facing dune, shuffled into the sand). Note the time of day that the snake was located.

COLOUR

The colour of the snake should never be the only criteria used to identify it. Many different species share surprisingly similar colours and patterns. Similarly, individuals of the same species may differ greatly from one another in colour. Arabian cobras are a good example of this, where you may find specimens ranging from yellow to dark brown in the same area.

Colour should always be noted, but used in conjunction with other features.

Finer Details

In the section dealing with specific snakes, information on the aforementioned basic characteristics is included. In addition to this, more specific information such as scale positioning and scale counts are given. Initially, it may all seem very confusing and unnecessary, but it may be these details that will assist you in telling very similar looking snakes apart. Some sea snakes, for example, look quite similar to one another, but all have their own unique combination of head, and body scales to tell them apart.

Another useful application of scale counting is where one encounters the sloughed skin of a snake in the field. These have little or no colour, but can easily be identified by looking at scale patterns and numbers. A mere fragment of the snake can be used to identify a badly damaged road-killed snake or one partially consumed by a predator.

HEAD SCALES

Looking at position, number, presence or absence of certain scales on the head has long been an accepted way of accurately identifying different species, and subspecies of snakes. Figures 7 and 8 show labeled diagrams of the head scales found on most snakes. Although most snakes can be identified without looking at such fine detail, some require a double check, just to make sure. If the structure of the head scales is an important identification criterion, then this will be mentioned under the 'Details', and 'Diagnostic Features' heading of each species.

Fig 7. Head scales of a typical snake.

ro - rostral scale
na - nasal scale
lo - loreal scale
up - upper labial scale
ll - lower labial scale
po - post-ocular scale
su - supra-ocular scale
pa - parietal scale
do - dorsal scale
fr - frontal scale
me - mental scale
as - anterior sublingual scales
ps - posterior sublingual scales

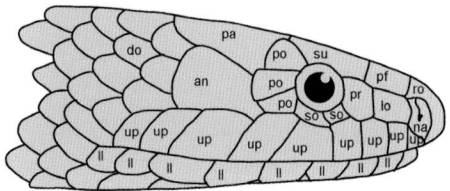

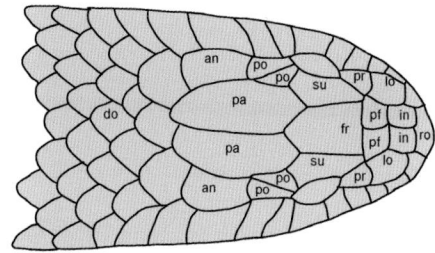

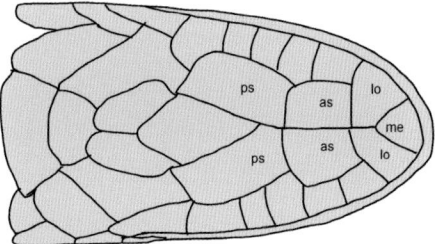

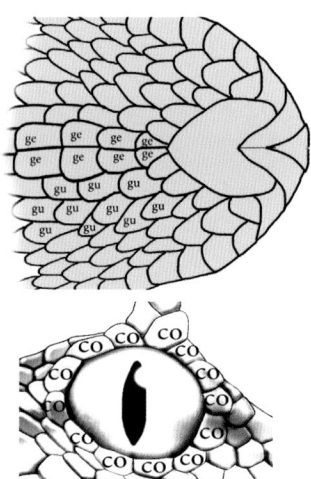

Fig 8. Other scales present on certain snakes.

gu - gular scales
ge - genial scales
co - circum-orbital scales

39

How to Identify Snakes

DORSAL SCALES

The dorsal scales cover the back and sides of the snake, and are generally small and uniform. Included under the general information for individual snakes, is a mid-body scale count. This is a technique used to determine the number of dorsal scale rows present on that snake. Counting scales at close quarters should only be attempted on dead snakes, or on sloughed skins. Fig 9 shows how to take an accurate mid-body scale count. Normally one would start with a dorsal scale joining a ventral scale at midbody and start counting forward diagonally up to the spine, and diagonally back down the other side.

Apart from the number of dorsal scales, the pattern the scales lie in and the shape of the scales themselves can often be a giveaway as to the species.

Fig 10 shows the different types of dorsal scales present on Arabian snakes. Generally burrowing snakes have glossy smooth scales, which do not overlap strongly. This prevents sand and dirt from accumulating on, and between scales. Many of the snakes that rely on camouflage in order to catch prey, have keeled scales. These scales give the snake a more broken up appearance, and if, in the case of horned vipers for example, the snake should partially bury itself in the sand, the little ridges along each scale will help to keep a certain

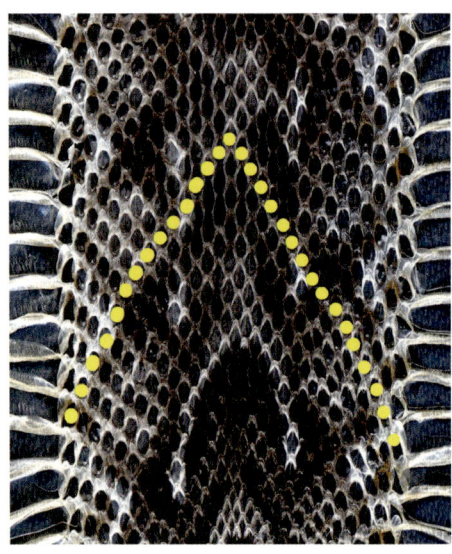

Fig 9. A dorsal scale count made on the sloughed skin of a snake. This snake has a mid-body scale count of 31.

amount of sand on the snake's body, thus rendering it more invisible. Many venomous, and non-venomous snakes alike use their roughly keeled scales to create a rasping sound when rubbed together. This acts as a form of warning. The most dramatically keeled scales belong to male short sea snakes. These form a spine in mature specimens.

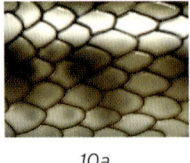
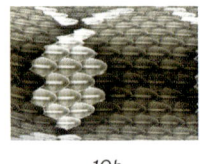

10a   10b   10c

Fig 10. a – smooth dorsal scales; b – keeled dorsal scales; c – spinose dorsal scales.

VENTRAL SCALES

These are on the belly or the ventral surface. They usually take the form of large shiny plates and are used to protect the belly, and to assist locomotion in terrestrial snakes. As they overlap, pointing backwards, they assist in gaining traction on the ground, and are the perfect compromise between protection and flexibility. Sea snakes have very small ventrals as they do not crawl around, but rather swim whereas puff adders have large, well developed ventrals to cope with the amount of wear and tear inflicted on the scales as a result of the force of gravity from the bulky body. Thread snakes don't have visible ventral scales, as they live underground.

ANAL AND SUBCAUDAL SCALES

The anal scale occurs directly behind the last ventral scale. It usually takes the form of a small plate, or flap, protecting the soft tissue of the cloacal opening. Anal scales may be entire (Fig 11a) or divided (Fig 11b). Subcaudal scales are the ventral scales of the tail. They too can be divided in some species and entire in others.

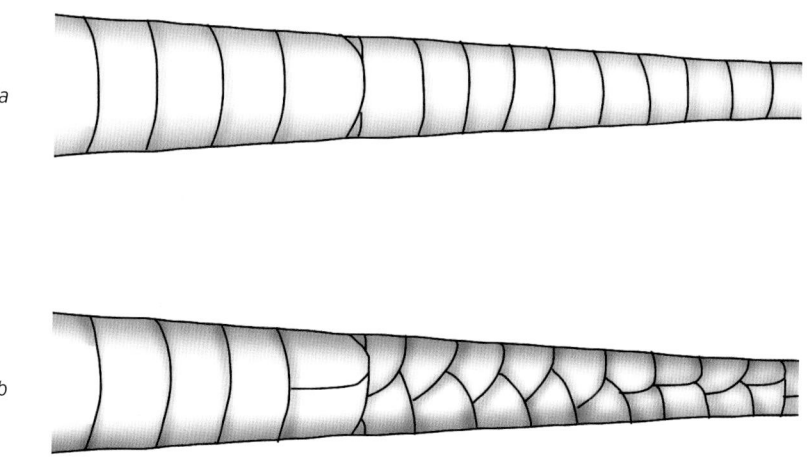

11a

11b

Fig 11. This diagram illustrates the underside of the tail and cloacal region. 11a - entire anal and subcaudal scales; 11b - divided anal and subcaudal scales.

Signs and Tracks

Snakes are not often encountered in the wild but most will leave some evidence of their presence. Sandy deserts make snake tracks easy to spot, as do dirt roads and soft mud. Sloughed skins found in the field can be used to accurately identify snakes. Snake faeces, although rarely encountered, is quite unique in composition and can easily be identified as such, although identifying individual species from faecal material would be largely impossible.

Snake tracks left in substrate such as sand or soil are best observed in the early morning. At this time the sun is low and casts long shadows on the tracks, highlighting small details. Many snakes are nocturnal, so the tracks from the previous night's activity will be relatively fresh in the morning condensation. As soon as the sun comes out, the sand will dry up and the wind will distort the tracks.

Is it a Snake?

Worm lizard tracks.

Many other animals, and wind-blown objects, will leave impressions in the sand that might, at first glance, resemble snake tracks. Worm lizards flop around the desert in wild spasmic movements that leave tracks similar to side-winding snakes. Lizards may drag tails or leave belly-scale impressions in the substrate. In these cases the obvious thing to look for is the presence of footprints. Leaves blowing in the wind can leave very deceptive trails that look quite snake-like at times. Ants use regular 'highways' across the desert, which, in time, form smooth, winding trails that may easily be mistaken for snake tracks. The fact that they do not undulate regularly, yet leave no scale impressions on the sand, should lead one to the right conclusion.

Identifying Snakes by their Tracks

Although some snakes are virtually impossible to distinguish from looking at their tracks, many are quite distinct and very easily identified. Terrestrial snakes generally follow one of four forms of locomotion. To identify these will bring us one step closer to identifying the species. Criteria such as range, habitat and time of day (if tracks are very fresh) can then be used to get a more specific idea.

RECTILINEAR MOVEMENT

This type of movement is utilized by heavy-bodied snakes. It involves the snake moving in a straight line using the moveable ribs and interstitial muscles to propel the body forward, much like the legs of a millipede. The ventral scales, pointing backwards, will gain purchase on the substrate. These snakes will only adopt a more conventional, sepentine, type of locomotion if disturbed.

The only snakes to regularly adopt rectilinear motion in Arabia are the Field's horned viper and the puff adder. The tracks are distinctive in that they are straight, wide and maintain impressions of ventral scale detail, which resembles the tread of a tiny tank. In the case of puff adders, a thinner furrow often runs down the middle of the main track; this is the impression of the tail being dragged behind the body. Females often lift the tail and drop it to the ground again, creating an irregular squiggling pattern.

Puff adder tracks. In this case, the heavy continuous drag mark left by the tail indicates that the snake is a male.

SERPENTINE MOVEMENT

This is the typical movement of snakes and involves the snake following an undulating path. It is seldom that the body follows the exact path of the head; so serpentine snake tracks tend to be smudged and inconsistent. This is more evident on difficult surfaces or when the snake is moving uphill. Sand snakes, especially young specimens, tend to form neat single serpentine tracks, but generally this is restricted to very light bodied snakes. The tracks of most snakes adopting serpentine movement retain little or no scale detail, as the ventral scales are being dragged across the sand. Ventral, and lower dorsal scale impressions can be noted in areas where the snake has stopped for a while, or perhaps struggled with a prey animal. Snake tracks commonly observed that employ a serpentine form of locomotion include

Signs and Tracks

all slender to moderately slender snakes. At points of obstruction, all snakes may adopt a concertina-like position where the body is bunched up in S-shaped coils and the posterior section is anchored while the rest of the body is pushed forward.

SIDE-WINDING

This form of locomotion is restricted to stout-bodied desert vipers such as saw-scaled vipers and horned vipers. It is a perfect adaptation for negotiating soft sand dunes. The snake positions the body in a loose S-shape and leads with the head and neck. The body then follows to create a track diagonal to the direction in which the snake is moving. Each part of the ventral surface will touch the sand without dragging, so scale detail on fresh tracks is clear. The snake will continue throwing coils forward thus creating rows of short diagonal lines or S-shapes. Most Arabian desert-dwelling sidewinders are geographically

Left & bottom: *Malpolon tracks showing irregular sepentine patterns, typical of moderately slender species.*

Below: *Tracks made by a baby sand snake. Only the lightest-bodied snakes leave a uniform undulating track.*

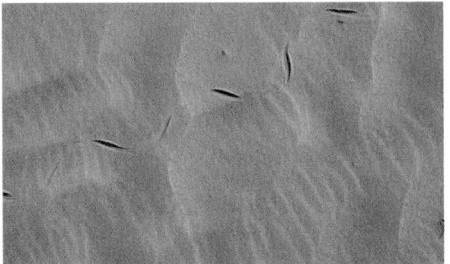

separated and are thus easy to identify. Horned vipers overlap the range of other sidewinders, but have high ventral scale detail and a medial ridge that bisects the ventral surface.

FOSSORIAL LOCOMOTION

It is hard to define this as a particular type of locomotion. Species such as thread snakes, flowerpot snakes, Revoil's short snakes and sand boas will push around in loose substrate and will often do so just beneath the surface creating a track that looks like a miniature plough has been run through the spot. Many species will surface occasionally leaving behind a more conventional, usually serpentine track. Be cautious when assessing tracks like this as many beetles also shuffle around just below the sand surface, as do worm lizards, sandfish (skinks) and a host of other desert creatures.

Above: *Typical side-winding tracks left by a saw-scaled viper.*

Left: *Side-winding tracks made by an Arabian horned viper. Horned viper tracks can be identified by high scale detail and the presence of a medial ridge on the tracks.*

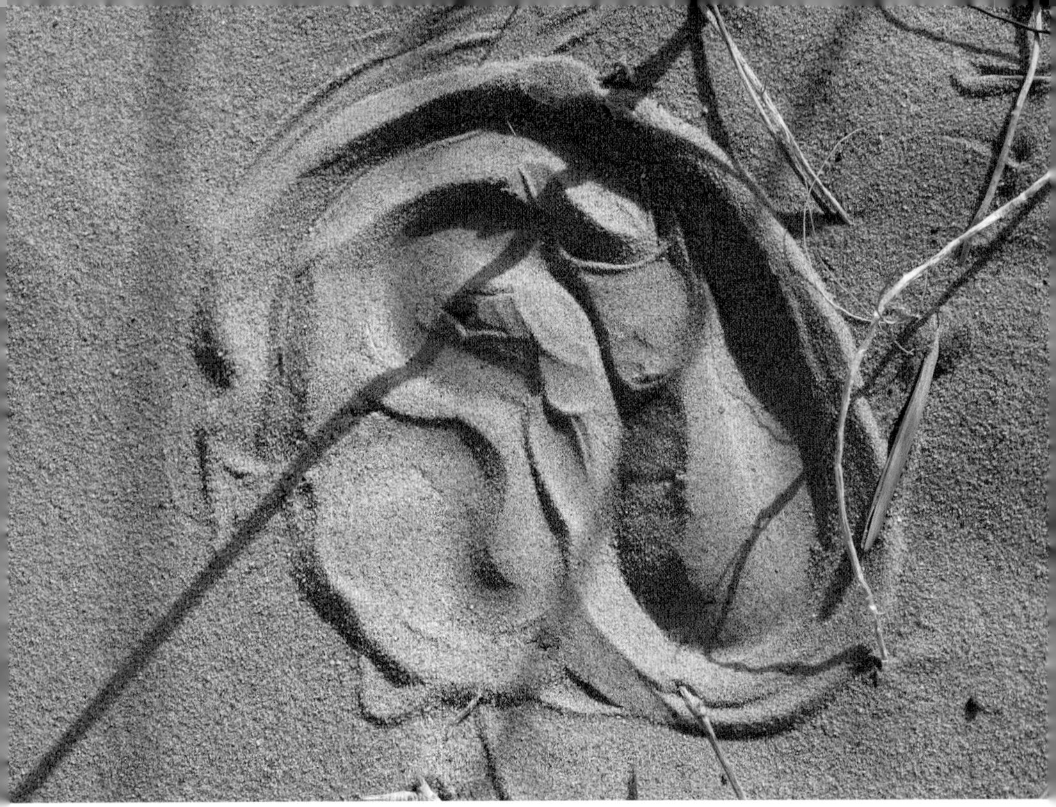

Above: *An impression made by an Arabian horned viper after it shimmied into the sand to wait in ambush.*

Below: *Tracks made by a sand boa. On the right, it employed a serpentine form of locomotion and then started to burrow towards the left.*

SLOUGHED SKINS

All snakes slough, or shed their skins as they grow and these are left behind wherever the snake happened to be at the time. As most snakes feel quite vulnerable during the sloughing process, many will choose to retire underground or in other recesses until they have rid themselves of the old skin. It is therefore most common to find the skins of tree-dwelling species and quite rare to find those of terrestrial species.

Sloughed skins are usually transparent with a faint impression of the snake's patterns on the skin. The scales on the snake's head and body are the most important identification tools. Look at the formation of the head scales and the size of the eyes (the brilles, or eye scales, are shed with the rest of the skin). Look at the shape, pattern, number and texture of the dorsal and ventral scales.

Mid-body dorsal scale row counts are especially useful when just part of a sloughed skin is found. The easiest technique for doing this is to remove a length of the skin and slit it down the ventral surface. Lay the skin flat and start a diagonal scale count as shown in Fig 9. Some shed skins retain shape and pattern very well and are quite easy to identify, but all distort to some level and appear larger than the snake that produced them and therefore cannot be used to measure the length of a snake.

The sloughed skin of an Oman carpet viper.

FAECES

Snake faeces are unique in many respects. They are usually accompanied by a block of uric acid in the form of a white, pinkish or greenish gel, or chalky substance. The actual faecal material consists of tightly packed hair, in the case of rodent-eating snakes, and scales, beetle exoskeletons or other invertebrate matter in the case of lizard eaters. Snakes that consume toads or frogs produce smaller faecal packages usually laden with insect remains. Monitor lizard faeces closely resemble snake faeces and are very difficult to tell apart. Spiny-tailed lizards, foxes, cats and birds can all produce similar looking stools, but either lack the uric acid mass (Spiny-tailed lizard, fox, cat etc), or do not have solid indigestible material in the stool, as in birds, which would regurgitate this as a casting. Although one can speculate as to the species of snake responsible, it is almost impossible to be certain of this.

A wadi racer swallowing a fish. These snakes will eat any small vertebrates.

When using this guide to identify a snake, the first step is to simply look at the illustrations and colour photographs. Use the identification criteria mentioned in the previous chapter to match the snake with an illustration. The top and profile illustrations are accurate representations of head scalation. It is important to note however, that often the scales on the head of the specimen being examined will not match the illustration perfectly, as snakes are not identical to each other, so look at the placement of scales mentioned as identification features and allow for a little leeway on the size, shape and exact positioning. The small colour illustrations, although anatomically proportionate, are provided only to show the body shape, and different common colour variations of that species. Colour photographs have been included where available as cross reference.

Information is given in a standardized form for each snake dealt with in this book. It is formatted in a manner whereby quick identification is easy. By highlighting the physical features under the column 'Details', and those characteristics most practical for specific identification under 'Diagnostic Features', the most important facts can be obtained without the reader being bogged down with other information.

Some species closely resemble others within the same range. The most basic differences between the species in question and those that resemble it are outlined under the title 'Possible Confusion'. If more information is required, this can be sought in the pages dealing with similar species.

The text and maps providing information on distribution are only as comprehensive as the amount of data that has been made available to present. Although they are drawn from information on specimens plotted by scientists over several decades, new localities are still regularly reported. With this in mind, if a snake is found outside the range indicated in this book, do not rule it out. It is possible that remnant populations of certain species occur away from the main population.

A baby puff adder.

ADDITIONAL INFORMATION ON NATURAL HISTORY

Often information such as the habitat that a snake was discovered in will give further clues as to what species it is. For example, a small viper in the north of Oman that rasps its scale together when disturbed could be one of two species, either the Oman carpet viper, or the Sindh saw-scaled viper. If the snake was discovered in the sandy plains, it was probably the latter, as the former is normally only associated with mountains and wadis, and Sindh saw-scaled vipers almost never enter true mountain habitat.

Some snakes may also reveal their identity through specific behavioural patterns. For example, a snake that spreads a hood and confronts one when disturbed would almost certainly be a cobra, whereas one that spreads a hood but faces the attacker with the back of the hood could well be a malpolon. Certain snakes, such as desert black snakes may hiss loudly while similar looking species such as

burrowing asps, might hide their head as a means of defence.

Other information under the 'Natural History' title, such as reproduction is included where available and is more for general interest.

QUESTIONABLE SPECIES

A small icon (below right) has been placed to the right of the common name of snakes that may have been erroneously recorded from Arabia in literature. As the contrary has not been proven, they are still included in this book.

NOTE: To the right of each scientific name is the authority responsible for describing the species and the year in which it was identified. Brackets indicate the scientific name of the species has been revised since then.

Flowerpot Snake

Rhamphotyphlops braminus   *(Daudin, 1803)*

 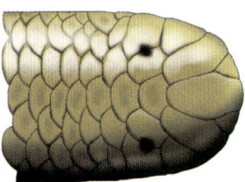

Description

Flowerpot snakes reach a maximum total length of around 17 cm but are more commonly 12–15 cm as adults. The head is rounded and almost indiscernible from the body. The small mouth is placed well under the head. The eyes are near vestigial and are visible only as dark patches under the head scales.

The body is extremely slender and cylindrical, with very little taper from head to tail. It is more or less round in section. The tail is indistinct and is only slightly longer than the width, terminating in a conical spine. Body scales are plate-like, very smooth and imbricate without much contour.

Flowerpot snakes vary in colour. In Arabia uniform pinkish specimens are most often seen. Elsewhere, tan, dark brown or blackish specimens occur. Lighter specimens tend to have darker-edged scales, giving a net appearance. They usually have a pale tail tip and some specimens have pale snout, cloacal and tail regions (not recorded in Arabia as yet).

Details

Mid-body scale rows: 20 (from suture to suture around entire body)
Subcaudals: Indistinct
Ventrals: No visible ventrals
Head scales: Nasal divided or partially divided; rostral narrow; supraoculars oblique and larger than prefrontal; 4 upper labials, 1st in contact with nasal, 2nd in contact with nasal and preocular, 3rd in contact with preocular and ocular, 4th with ocular; head shield sutures with pale glands

Diagnostic Features

- Fairly slender, shiny, worm-like snake
- Tail same length or slightly longer than width
- Tail ends in conical spine
- Eyes present beneath the junction of two scales

Possible Confusion

Young specimens are similar to thread snakes (*Leptotyphlops*). Thread snakes are proportionately thinner. All Arabian thread snakes have protruding snouts, whereas the head of *Rhamphotyphlops* is completely rounded. Arabian species of thread snakes have eyes under a single scale and not under the junction of two scales, as with the flowerpot snake.

Distribution

This is the most widespread terrestrial snake in the world. In Arabia it has been recorded from various localities throughout the peninsula and almost certainly exists in agricultural areas across the region. It is commonly introduced from Central Asia and elsewhere with potted plants and growing media.

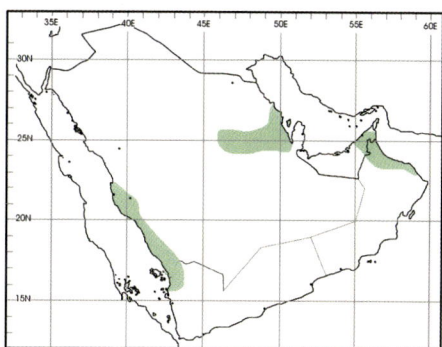

Natural History

Flowerpot snakes feed on termites and their larvae. They lead a completely fossorial existence and are only seen during heavy rains or if excavated.

They are known to reproduce through parthenogenesis (ability to reproduce without being fertilized by a male), hence the high rate of colonization worldwide.

Although the small eyes are sensitive to light and dark, they are of little further use to the snake.

They almost always occur in areas with a high rate of natural ground moisture, or (more commonly in Arabia) in artificially watered, cultivated land.

A dark specimen of the flowerpot snake photographed in Papua New Guinea.

Large-snouted Thread Snake

Leptotyphlops macrorhynchus macrorhynchus   *(Jan, 1860)*

 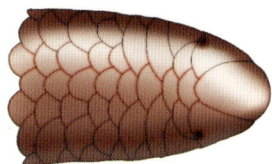

Description

Large-snouted thread snakes reach a maximum length of 26.9 cm (Iran), but are more commonly 15-20 cm in total length. The head is indistinguishable from the body and terminates in a hooked snout. The eyes are vestigial and appear as dark patches beneath the head scales. The body is extremely slender with virtually no tapering, giving the snake an earthworm-like appearance. The tail is indistinct, tapers abruptly right at the tip and constitutes about 8% of the total length.

Most recorded specimens are a uniform pink, or flesh-coloured. Younger specimens appear slightly translucent, with visible blood vessels beneath the skin.

Details

Mid-body scale rows: 297-437 (total number)
Scale rows at mid-tail: 10
Anal: Entire, prominent
Subcaudals: 33-48, almost indistinguishable from dorsals
Head scales: Rostral extends almost to the level of the eyes; ocular extends to the lip bordered by a labial on either side; anterior upper labial touches the much larger intraocular, but does not make contact with the ocular

Diagnostic Features

- Tiny, pinkish worm-like snake
- Hooked snout

Species Identification Guide

Possible Confusion

Flowerpot snakes, *Rhamphotyphlops braminus* closely resemble thread snakes. They are slightly more robust in form and the head is more distinct, being marginally broader than the neck. In flowerpot snakes, the eye is situated beneath the skin at the junction of two head scales, whereas the thread snake has eyes situated beneath the ocular scale.

Distribution

In Arabia they occur in scattered localities in the entire mountain periphery, and the central regions around Riyadh. This snake is probably inadvertently distributed to many new localities each year by stowing away in plant pots and agricultural medium.

Elsewhere, they are known from West Africa to Pakistan and north to Turkey.

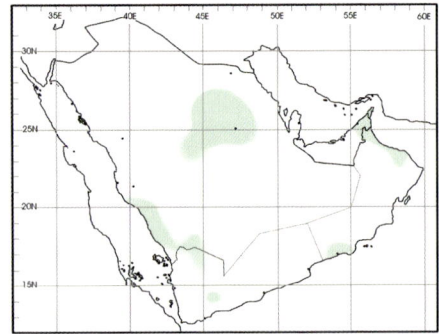

Natural History

Known to feed on ants and their larvae, thread snakes are entirely fossorial, only generally found if excavated, or during rain.

They are most commonly found in agricultural land that is well irrigated.

Above & following: A juvenile large-snouted thread snake from Al Dhaid, UAE.

Nurse's Thread Snake

Leptotyphlops nursii   *(Anderson, 1896)*

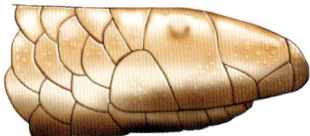
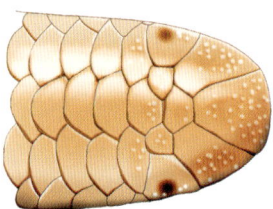

Description

Nurse's thread snakes are known to reach around 25 cm in total length. The neck region is thinner than the head, making it slightly distinct. The snout is elongated with a distinct 'overbite' if viewed from the side. The eyes are near-vestigial and present as dark patches under the head scales. The body is very slender and worm-like and is round in section.

The tail is indistinct, only tapering very near to the tip, and constitutes around 10% of the total length.

Most specimens from Arabia appear to be a uniform pink colour. Another morph on record includes a light grey-brown dorsum, with a whitish or yellow ventrum.

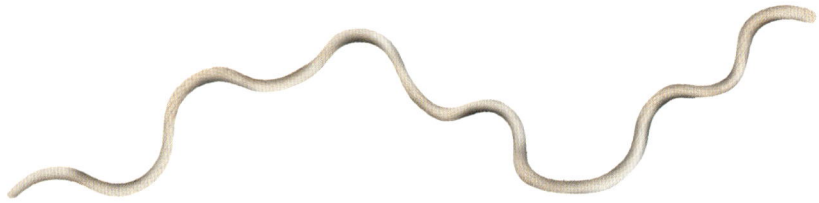

Details

Mid-body scale rows: 14, from margin to margin, smooth
Total dorsal scales: 281-375
Mid-tail scale rows: 12
Total dorsal scales on tail: 32-48
Head scales: Rostral broader than nasal, does not meet the level of eyes; nasal divided; nostril removed from nasal; 1st labial very small with parallel upper and lower margins; ocular on labial margin; supraocular and frontal shields nearly equal

Diagnostic Features

- Tiny, pink worm-like snake with long rounded snout
- Rostral scale moderate width and does not reach the level of the eyes

Possible Confusion

Nurse's thread snakes resemble most other thread snakes at a glance. They are characterized by the long, unhooked snout, and a rostral scale, the apex of which, falls short of the level of the eyes. They differ from flowerpot snakes, *Rhamphotyphlops braminus* in having eyes beneath the central part of a scale as opposed to being on the suture of two scales.

Distribution

Found in scattered localities in the Asir Mountains, south to Yemen and east to the western limit of the Hadramaut Range. Two specimens have been recorded in Oman, not far from the vicinity of Muscat. The full extent of their range is unknown.

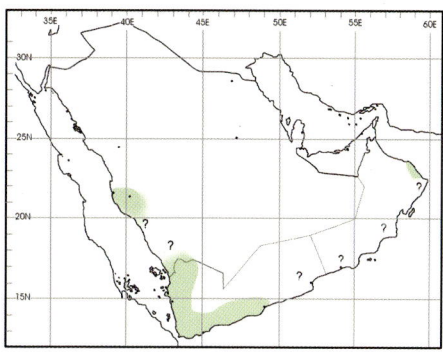

Natural History

Very little is known of the habits of this species. They feed on ant larvae and are completely fossorial. A small number (2 or 3) of thin-shelled eggs are laid that only take a matter of days to hatch.

A Nurse's thread snake collected in Dibdab, Oman.

Buri's Thread Snake

Leptotyphlops burii   *(Boulenger, 1905)*

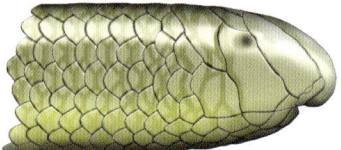 

Description

Buri's thread snakes reach around 20 cm. The head is indistinguishable from the body and terminates in a blunt, round, but slightly protruding snout. Head scales are shiny and without contour. Eyes are near-vestigial and appear as dark patches under the head scales. The body is very slender, does not taper throughout the length, and is round in section. The tail is indistinct, tapers abruptly at the end and constitutes around 6 or 7% of the total length.

Known specimens are brownish above and yellow on the ventral surface, with a faint lace-like pattern mimicking the body scales.

Details

Mid-body scales: 14, smooth
Total scale rows: 403-408
Mid-tail scale rows: 12
Anal: Entire
Subcaudals: 28-33
Head scales: Rostral broad and distinct, extending to between the eyes; nasal divided and in contact with prefrontal; supraocular slightly larger than frontal; the ocular extends to the lip, surrounded by a labial on either side (large behind and very small in front); occipitals divided

Diagnostic Features

- Tiny brown snake with yellow ventrum that looks like a worm
- Divided occipitals, total dorsals over 400

Possible Confusion

They are similar to other species of thread snakes and flowerpot snakes, *Rhamphotyphlops braminus*. Buri's thread snakes are much more slender than flowerpot snakes with the eye under a single scale rather than at the junction of two scales. They differ from large-snouted thread snakes in that they lack the beak-like protrusion. Nurse's thread snakes have a lower total dorsal scale count (less than 375 as opposed to more than 400 of *L. burii*).

Distribution

Known from one locality in south-western Yemen.

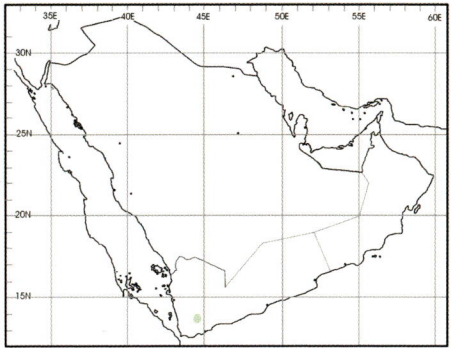

Natural History

Nothing is known about the natural history of this rare species. Presumably it shares similar habits with other *Leptotyphlops* (ie, fossorial and feeds on ant larvae).

Species Identification Guide

Javelin Sand Boa

Eryx jaculus jaculus   *(Hasselquist & Linnaeus, 1758)*

Description

Javelin sand boas may exceptionally reach 80 cm, but are more commonly about 50-60 cm in total length. The head and neck are indistinct. The head is less flattened than the other two Arabian sand boa species. The eyes are laterally placed and moderately small, with brown irises and elliptical pupils. The body is thick and the dorsal scales are very smooth and shiny. The ventrals are well developed. A small spur exists on either side of the anal opening. These are larger in males. The tail is conical and constitutes about 7 or 8% of the total length.

The base colour may be sandy brown, yellowish or dull orange. There may be dark brown bars, blotches or transverse rectangles on the dorsal surface. These patterns break up towards the flanks. A single row of widely spaced dark spots extends along the length of either flank, close to the junction of ventral and dorsal scales. Another morph includes large roundish, dark-edged spots alternating on the dorsum and breaking up on the flanks. The ventral surface is white or cream.

Details

Mid-body scale rows: 40-51, smooth
Anal: Entire
Subcaudals: 15-34, entire
Ventrals: 165-200
Head scales: 7-14 circum-orbital scales; 5-9 inter-orbital scales

Diagnostic Features

- 5-9 inter-orbital scales
- Tail ends obtusely
- Laterally placed eyes
- Spurs present on either side of anal opening

Possible Confusion

Jayakar's sand boa, *Eryx jayakari* may share part of its range. The eyes of the javelin sand boa are placed on the side of the head, those of the Jayakar's sand boa are on top. The tail of *E. jaculus* ends bluntly, whereas that of *E. jayakari* ends in a spike.

Distribution

North-eastern Saudi Arabia. Elsewhere, it is known from Mediterranean Europe, North Africa, western Asia, Syria, Jordan, Iraq, Iran, eastern Europe and as far east as China.

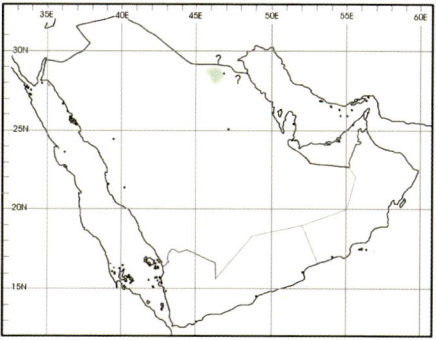

Natural History

They live in sandy areas and areas with loose soil. Not restricted to desert, javelin sand boas reside in rodent burrows and under stones as well as burrowing in the sand.

They feed primarily on lizards and rodents, but birds and even snails have been recorded as prey. Cannibalism has been recorded in captivity.

More active than most sand boas, *E. jaculus* is a spirited forager as well as an ambush hunter. Rodents are probably most frequently caught after being blocked inside burrows. They are powerful constrictors.

Unlike the Jayakar's sand boa, javelin sand boas are capable of living in a variety of habitats, and are better adapted than *E. jayakari* for life above ground, having larger ventral scales and a more slender body.

Above & below: A captive, adult javelin sand boa from unknown locality.

Egyptian Sand Boa
Eryx colubrinus   (Hasselquist & Linnaeus, 1758)

Description

Egyptian sand boas may exceptionally reach 80 cm, but are more commonly 50-60 cm in total length. The head is blunt and indistinct from the body. The eyes are small and are situated laterally. The pupils are elliptical. The body is very thick. Dorsal scales are small, smooth and shiny. The tail is distinct and quite stubby, with a conical scale on the tip. A spur can be seen on either side of the cloacal opening; this is much larger in males. The tail constitutes around 8-10% of the total length.

The base colour is yellowish or grey with large, dark brown, irregular spots on the dorsal surface. The colouration on the head and the lower flanks break up on some specimens to become quite cryptic. The ventral surface can be white, cream or yellow.

Details

Mid-body scale rows: 47-53
Anal: Entire
Subcaudals: 19-28, entire
Ventrals: 171-197, narrow
Head scales: 11-13 inter-orbital scales

Species Identification Guide

Diagnostic Features

- Short, very fat snake with large round spots on dorsum and indistinct neck
- 11-13 inter-orbital scales
- Tail terminates in conical scale
- Prominent spurs on either side of anal opening

Possible Confusion

The Arabian distribution of this snake is largely unknown (if it is indeed extant in the area). It may share habitat with the Arabian sand boa, *Eryx jayakari*. Arabian sand boas have upward pointing eyes and a smoother skin. The pattern of *E. jayakari* is generally less bold, following the contours of the scales, whereas the Egyptian sand boa has a 'polka-dot' appearance. The tail of *E. jayakari* terminates in a spike, not a conical scale as in *E. colubrinus*.

Distribution

In Arabia, it is only known from one specimen allegedly collected in western Yemen. In Africa, it occurs from the Nile Delta in Egypt, south to northern Kenya.

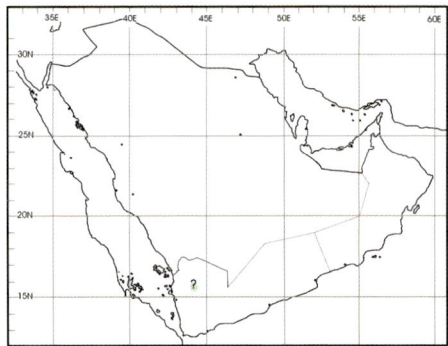

Natural History

They occur in semi-arid to arid conditions, usually in loose sandy soil. Occasionally they shelter under stones and logs etc, or can be found in leaf litter or at the base of shrubs and grass tussocks.

   The young feed heavily on geckos. Adults will take rodents, lizards and ground-nesting birds. As with all members of the *Bioidae* family, Egyptian sand boas are powerful constrictors. They have even rows of very sharp teeth for grasping. They will bite if provoked.

   Egyptian sand boas give birth to 3-7 babies in early summer.

Above & below: *Adult Egyptian sand boas from Egypt.*

Arabian Sand Boa

Eryx jayakari   *Boulenger, 1888*

Description

Arabian sand boas may exceptionally reach 64 cm, but are more commonly around 30–45 cm in total length. The head is small and indistinct from the body and is covered in small fragmented scales. The snout is spade-shaped. The eyes are situated on the top of the head, are orange, with yellow-rimmed elliptical pupils. The body is short and thick, and roundish in section (although sand boas can flatten themselves at will). Dorsal scales are small and smooth. A small spur exists on either side of the cloacal opening. These are much larger in males. The ventral scales are narrow. The stout, conical tail constitutes about 6 or 7% of the total length.

The base colour is yellow, orange or tan. The dorsal surface is barred with reddish brown, brown or blackish transverse bars. These bars may or may not split on the vertebral line and alternate each other in a rough checkered pattern. The edges of the body patterns follow the sutures of the dorsal scales, rather than cutting through them. The head is speckled and blotched in browns and black. The ventral surface is white, cream or light pink.

Details

Mid-body scale rows: 37–51
Preanal: entire and small
Subcaudals: 16–25, entire
Ventrals: 158–184, narrow
Head scales: Fragmented and small; 11 upper labials; 9 or 10 scales surrounding eyes; 4 or 5 scales separating eyes

Diagnostic Features

- Small, upward-facing, elevated eyes
- 4 or 5 inter-orbital scales
- 9 or 10 circum-orbital scales
- Tail terminates in a small spike

Possible Confusion

It is possible that the range of the Arabian sand boa overlaps that of the javelin sand boa, *Eryx jaculus* in the north-east and the Egyptian sand boa, *E. colubrinus* in the south-west. Both these species have laterally placed eyes, whereas *E. jayakari* have dorsally placed eyes.

Distribution

Widespread. Present in suitable habitat throughout the Arabian Peninsula. Absent from much of north-western Saudi Arabia, the central regions of the Rub al-Khali and all mountain ranges.

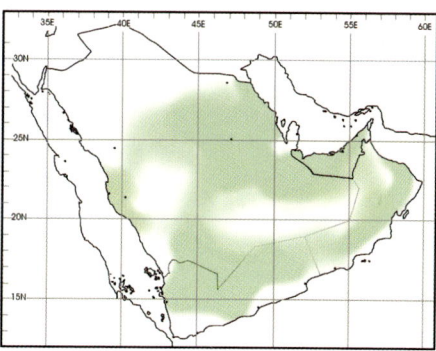

Natural History

Arabian sand boas inhabit sandy desert and probably penetrate further into the great sands of the Rub al-Khali than any other snake species.

They are usually quite deep in the sand during the day rising to just below the surface at night to lie in wait for prey, with only the raised eyes above the surface. Prey is killed by constriction.

A wide variety of prey is eaten. Neonates are known to eat soft-bodied invertebrates and young geckos. Juveniles and adults feed heavily on ground geckos as well as occasional rodents or shrews.

Sand boas mate on the surface. A small number of large eggs (usually less than four) are laid in early summer. Hatchlings emerge after around 60 days and average about 22 cm in total length.

Above: *Deep orange Arabian sand boa (Sharjah).*

Below: *Typical Arabian sand boa (Dubai).*

Hardwick's Rat Snake
Platyceps ventromaculatus   *(Gray, 1834)*

Description

Rat snakes reach a maximum length of around 95 cm, but adults of 65-70 cm are more common. The head is distinct and the eyes are large with pale brown irises and round pupils. The head is covered in large, smooth shields. The body and tail are very long and slender, with the tail constituting about 23-25% of the total body length. The body scales are smooth and shiny.

Several colour and pattern variations exist. Most commonly, the background colour is grey, brown or straw-coloured. A series of about 50 transverse black blotches runs along the back, fading towards the tail. The last-third of the body is without any pattern. A row of smaller dark spots runs along either flank, also fading. There may be a thick dark, diagonal stripe below each eye and another thicker one on the side of the head, terminating at the mouth. Often there is a prominent oblong marking starting on the back of the head, ending by merging with the first of the vertebral blotches. The underside is white or cream.

Details

Mid-body scale rows: 19, smooth
Anal: Divided
Subcaudals: 82-119
Ventrals: 194-211
Head scales: 8 upper labials with 4th and 5th entering the eye; 5 lower labials in contact with anterior chin shields

Species Identification Guide

Diagnostic Features

- Only banded *Platyceps sp.* within its Arabian distribution (except possibly UAE)
- Oblong neck spot
- 2 upper labials border the eye
- No posterior subocular

Possible Confusion

Although this species closely resembles the wadi racer, *Platyceps rhodorachus*, their ranges and habitats are generally exclusive within Arabia with the possible exception of the emirate of Abu Dhabi. Wadi racers have more than 214 ventrals, whereas rat snakes have a maximum of 211.

Distribution

Pakistan, Iran, Iraq, Kuwait. Within Arabia, it is known from north-eastern Saudi Arabia, Bahrain and a few of the islands off the United Arab Emirates. It is probably extant in many of the islands in the Arabian Gulf.

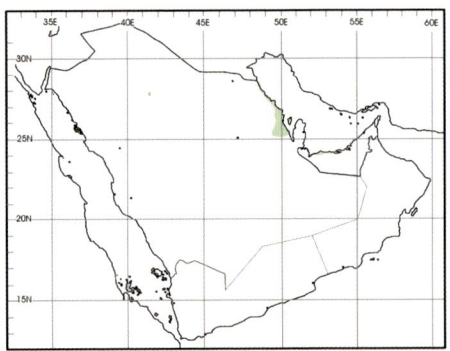

Natural History

Hardwick's rat snakes occupy marshes, vegetated desert and oases and prefer hard substrates.

They have adapted well to human settlements and are abundant in date groves, farm buildings, agricultural land and rubbish dumps.

Opportunistic, rat snakes will eat almost any small vertebrate. Young feed primarily on lizards (*Messalina, Acanthodactylus* etc). Adults feed heavily on mice and rats attracted by humans.

These are fast, alert, diurnal and active foragers that normally corner rodents down their holes, or chase after lizards. Prey is killed by chewing in oral secretions while the animal is restrained with coils of the body.

The primary means of defence is extreme speed in escaping, but should a rat snake be restrained, it will not hesitate to bite aggressively and painfully, simultaneously releasing a strong-smelling musky substance from its anal glands.

The saliva has some toxicity to small animals, but rat snakes are completely harmless to humans, with bites only resulting in mild itching.

Above & below: *Two adult rat snakes from Bahrain. Both colour morphs are common within the same region.*

Wadi Racer, Jan's Cliff Racer

Platyceps rhodorachus   *(Jan, 1865)*

Description

Adults may reach 128 cm but are more commonly around 60-70 cm. The head is moderate, distinct and covered in smooth large shields. The eyes are large with round pupils and dark brown irises. The snout is short and tapers to a round tip. The body and tail are long and extremely slender. The tail constitutes about 25-26% of the total length. The body scales are flat, smooth and shiny. The ventral scales are well developed.

Most wadi racers have a dorsal background colour of grey, tan or olive. The front half of the body is banded or checkered in a series of between 60 and 100 dark spots or bars, interspersed with light flecks. An alternating row of similar markings occurs on either flank. All markings fade towards the back half of the body. Ventral colour may be white, pink, yellow or, most commonly, cream.

Many other colour varieties of this snake exist in Arabia, from plain grey specimens with a single row of small dark grey spots on the flanks, to brick-red specimens, with or without the distinctive checkered pattern. Dark grey as well as black specimens are also known.

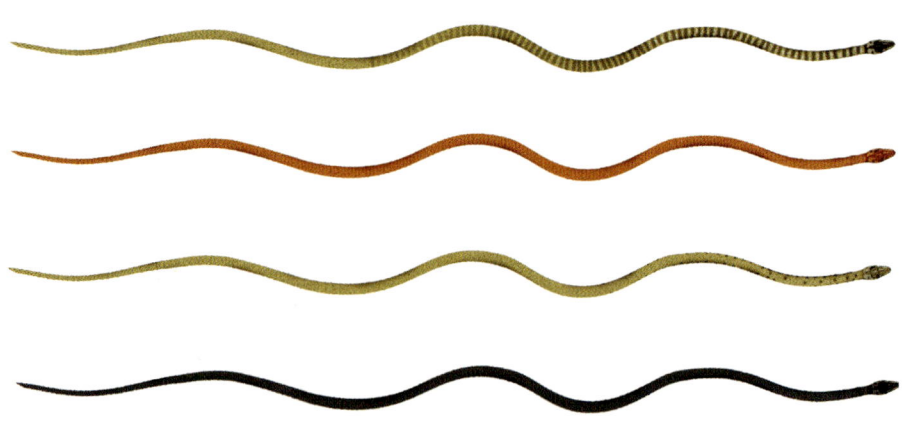

Details

Mid-body scale rows: 19
Anal: Divided
Subcaudals: 113-154, divided
Ventrals: 214-262
Head scales: 2 postoculars; 9 upper labials with 5th and 6th entering the eye; 4-5 lower labials

Diagnostic Features

- More than 111 subcaudals
- More than 210 ventrals
- Small, regular black blotches on the edges of the ventral scales

Possible Confusion

Hardwick's rat snakes, *Platyceps ventromaculatus* resemble wadi racers at a glance. Wadi racers have more than 214 ventral scales (compared to 211 of rat snakes) and are more slender. Generally the two species occupy exclusive habitats, but may overlap in parts of the UAE.

Distribution

Wadi racers are widespread in most mountainous areas throughout the region, from the north-west coast of Saudi Arabia, virtually around the entire coastline to the Musandam Peninsula. Also, most rocky or mountainous habitats in the interior. Elsewhere they are known from as far west as Libya, east across the Middle East, to Turkmenistan.

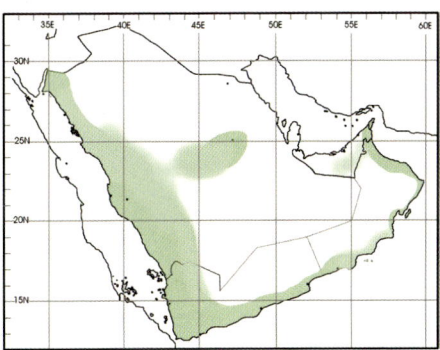

Natural History

Wadi racers are not dependent on water, but are attracted to it and lead a semi-aquatic lifestyle in wet areas. They live at all altitudes, in most mountain habitats as well as coastal plains and foothills.

They feed on most small vertebrates including lizards, amphibians, fish, rodents, shrews and other snakes, including their own kind. They avoid eating adult toads, but will avidly consume tadpoles.

Wadi racers are diurnal during the winter months and more crepuscular during summer,

avoiding the extreme daytime heat. They are extremely agile, fast snakes, employing this to good effect to elude predation. If restrained or cornered, they will strike out aggressively.

They are active hunters and can be observed checking cracks and holes systematically in search of prey. They even hunt in this manner underwater. Their eyesight is excellent and they are very sensitive to movement.

Prey succumbs to toxic saliva, after being 'chewed' upon for several seconds. They are not constrictors, but occasionally wind the body around the prey animal to control it.

Wadi racers are harmless to humans and bites result in mild itching for a short time.

Top: *A typical wadi racer from Khor Fakkan, UAE.*

Bottom: *A red wadi racer from Ta'izz, Yemen.*

Elegant Racer

Platyceps elegantissimus   *(Gunther, 1878)*

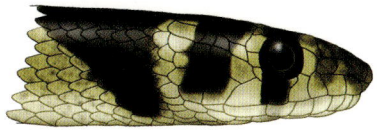

Description

Elegant racers may reach around 70 cm in total length, but are generally 50-60 cm. The head is proportionately large and distinct from the body. The snout is short and pointed. The head shields are flat and shiny. The eyes are large with round pupils, edged in gold. The irises are dark grey-brown. The body is moderately slender and is slightly laterally compressed in section. The tail is indistinct and constitutes about 23-24% of the total length.

The base colour is yellowish, tan or straw-coloured, with each dorsal scale edged in black. It is banded with 21-28 complete black rings, being thicker dorsally and thinner as they cross the ventral surface. Some specimens have a bright red or orange vertebral stripe along the entire length between the black bands. The ventral surface is whitish between the black/purple of the bands.

Details

Mid-body scale rows: 19, smooth
Anal: Divided
Subcaudals: 78-84, divided
Ventrals: 197-200, well developed
Head scales: 2 preoculars with upper in contact with frontal; 2 postoculars; 8 upper labials with 4th and 5th, or 5th entering the eye; 5 lower labials; anterior chin shields almost as long as posterior ones

Diagnostic Features

- Slender, petite snake with black bands and red vertebral stripe in some specimens
- Only snake with 21-28 complete black rings within the range covered in this book
- 19 mid-body scale rows

Possible Confusion

Due to distinctive pattern, they are not likely to be confused with other species within the region covered by this book. Wadi racers, *Platyceps rhodorachus* are more slender and have incomplete bands that fade towards the rear of the body.

Distribution

From Palestine and south-western Jordan, south-east to Riyadh and south to the northern limits of the Asir Mountains.

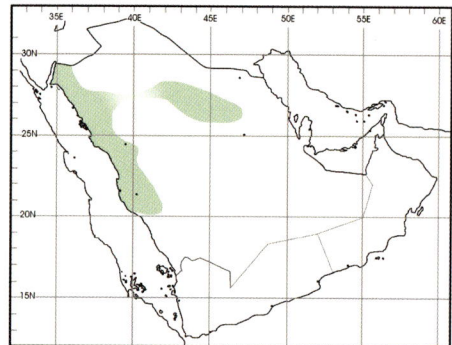

Natural History

Elegant racers occupy stony wadis, rocky hills and slopes. They find refuge under stones and down the unused burrows of other animals.

They probably feed on geckos and other lizards as well as young rodents.

Very little is known about this rare species. They are among the few racers to be partly nocturnal. They are extremely fast and agile.

An elegant racer with an orange vertebral stripe from Jordan.

Variable Racer

Platyceps variabilis   *(Boulenger, 1905)*

Description

Variable racers reach an average length of 35-40 cm. The head is moderate and is distinct from the body. The snout is shortened and tapers abruptly. The eyes are moderate with dark irises and round pupils. The body is moderately slender and round in section. The tail is indistinct and constitutes around 26-28% of the total length.

As the species name implies, this snake is variable in colour and pattern. The background colour may be grey, tan, reddish brown or orange. Some specimens have transverse bands or spots along the vertebral line and smaller alternating ones on the flanks. Others have no bars or spots, but a bright red vertebral stripe. Grey specimens with pale-edged scales exist, as do heavily banded ones. It would be difficult to use colour and pattern as an accurate form of diagnosis with this species.

Details

Mid-body scale rows: 17, smooth
Anal: Divided
Subcaudals: 80-90, divided
Ventrals: 155-169
Head scales: 8 upper labials with 4th and 5th entering eye; 8 lower labials with 4 or 5 in contact with the chin shields

Diagnostic Features

- 80-90 subcaudals
- 17 mid-body scale rows
- Only small *Platyceps* in this distribution that may have vertebral stripes

Possible Confusion

Specimens with vertebral striping may be confused with young sand snakes, *Psammophis schokari*. Sand snakes are much more slender with proportionately large heads and very large eyes. Young wadi racers, *Platyceps rhodorachus* may resemble banded specimens, but lack banding on the posterior half of the body, are more slender, and have a much higher ventral and dorsal scale counts.

Distribution

South-western Yemen highlands and Tihama.

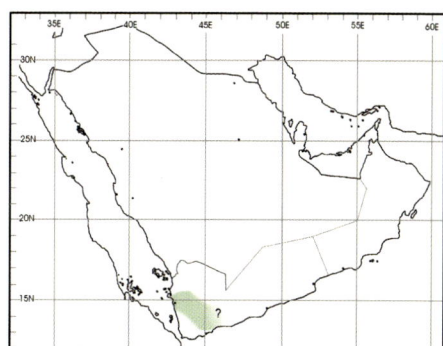

Natural History

Virtually nothing is known of the natural history of this species. It lives at high elevations under logs etc or down holes, are presumed to be nocturnal and probably feed on small vertebrates such as geckos and frogs.

They are oviparous, but nothing is known of their breeding cycle. Personal communication by the author with locals indicate that the species is common around Ta'izz, but becomes progressively more rare towards Sana'a.

Thomas' Racer

Platyceps thomasi   *(Parker, 1931)*

Description

Thomas' racers reach around 35–40 cm. The head is moderate, but distinct from the body. The snout is blunt and short. The eyes are moderate with a round pupil and dark iris. The body is fairly slender and round in section. Dorsal scales are smooth and flat with visible paired apical pits on each scale. The tail is indistinct and constitutes around 28% of the total body length.

The base colour is reddish brown, with the back of each dorsal scale edged in light grey. About 54 black bands extend down the length of the body. Although they enter the ventral area, they do not meet to form complete rings. A thick black band runs between the eyes and extends to the upper labials. A similar band lies parallel to this on the head and terminates at the mouth, just before the angle of the jaw. A third band forms a collar on the nape.

Details

Mid-body scale rows: 15, smooth with paired apical pits
Anal: Divided
Subcaudals: 79–82, divided
Ventrals: 156–160, well developed
Head scales: 8 upper labials with 4th and 5th entering eye; 9 lower labials with 4 in contact with chin shield

Diagnostic Features

- 33 bands on body and 22 on tail
- The only small, thin snake in its range that is banded from head to tail

Possible Confusion

Thomas' racers could only be confused with young specimens of the wadi racer, *Platyceps rhodorachus*. They are thicker set than wadi racers and are banded across the entire body and tail. Wadi racers, from the Dhofar region are usually only faintly banded on the anterior part of the body.

Distribution

Known from a few localities in Dhofar and eastern Yemen. It is unknown how far they might extend into Yemen.

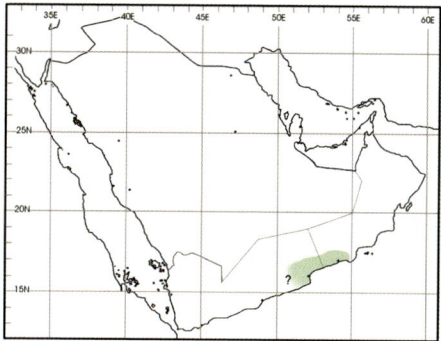

Natural History

Very little is known of the natural history of the Thomas' racer.

They have been found in well-vegetated mountainous areas above 200 m above sea level, as well as barren plateaus and coastal plain.

They probably feed on small geckos such as *Pristurus*, which are ubiquitous in Dhofar. Virtually nothing is known about this snake as only a few specimens are known to science. The physiology of the snake, and observations made by certain authors, suggests that it is an active diurnal hunter, but its close relatives, *P. manseri* and *P. variabilis* are presumed to be nocturnal.

The type-specimen of the Thomas' racer, collected in Dhofar, Oman.

Manser's Racer, Manser's Black Snake

Platyceps manseri   *(Leviton, 1986)*

 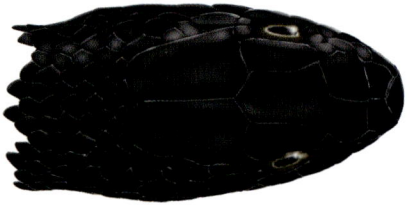

Description

Adults average around 42 cm in total length. The head is distinct and the eyes are large with round pupils. The irises are dark grey or brown. The snout is short, and tapers abruptly. The body is slender and oval in section, being slightly laterally compressed. Dorsal scales are smooth. The tail is indistinct and constitutes about 25% of the total body length.

Most commonly, the entire body is black with a blue-black ventral surface. Specimens with a black head and tan body with black-edged scales have also been found.

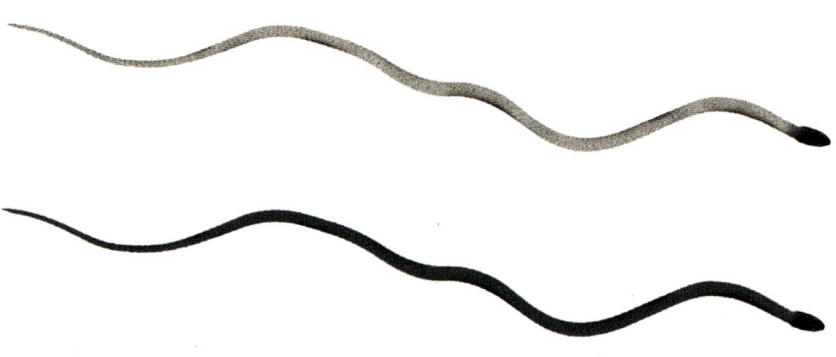

Details

Mid-body scale rows: 19, smooth
Anal: Divided
Subcaudal: 79-91, divided
Ventrals: 165-186
Head scales: 2 preoculars with lower one pushed between 3rd and 4th upper labials; 8 upper labials; 9 lower labials

Diagnostic Features

- Less than 190, and more than 165 ventral scales
- Frontal shield wider than supraocular
- 19 dorsal scale rows

Possible Confusion

They are similar in most respects to the variable racer, *P. variabilis*. Variable racers have a lower minimum ventral scale count (155), and 17 dorsal scale rows as opposed to 19 rows of *P. manseri*. Some authors have placed *P. manseri* as a subspecies of *P. variabilis*. *P. manseri* has only been recorded in the two colour forms mentioned, whereas *P. variabilis* has several colour and pattern variations.

Distribution

Manser's racers occur from the vicinity of Jizan in Saudi Arabia to Al Hudaidah in Yemen.

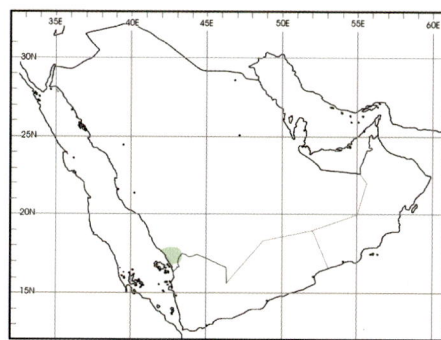

Natural History

Manser's racers apparently hide in caves and other dark recesses. They have been found in storm water drains and other man-made structures as well as rotting logs, brushheaps and rubbish dumps.

   They are thought to be, at least in part, insectivorous including cockroaches and crickets in the diet. They probably also feed on small vertebrates such as geckos.

   These snakes are only known from a handful of specimens. Virtually nothing is known of their biology, other than physical characteristics. They are presumed to be nocturnal.

Rhombic Egg Eater

Dasypeltis scabra   *(Linnaeus, 1758)*

Description

Egg eaters may exceptionally reach 105 cm but adults average 50-65 cm. The head is rounded, finger-shaped and is indistinct from the body. The eyes are large with pale golden irises and elliptical, cat-like pupils. The body is moderately slender, becoming stouter in older specimens. The body scales are heavily keeled and imbricate, with visible apical pits. Ventral scales are wide and well developed. The tail is indistinct and constitutes around 12-14% of the total length. Males have visible hemipenal bulges at the base of the tail.

The base colour is bluish grey, grey or brown with a series of dark rhomboid patches or squares along the back. These are interspaced with white, pinkish or yellow (most commonly white) patches. A series of dark transverse bands runs along either flank. There are prominent V-shaped markings on the nape of the neck, the points of which may reach the top of the head. The ventral surface may be white, cream or pink. It may or may not have slightly darker stippling. This is the typical patterning, but geographic variations probably exist in Arabia.

Details

Mid-body scale rows: 21-27, keeled with visible apical pits
Anal: Entire
Subcaudals: 38-78, divided
Ventrals: 180-243
Head scales: 1 preocular; 2 postoculars; posterior temporals keeled; 6-8 (usually 7) upper labials with 3rd and 4th, or 2nd and 3rd entering the eye; 7-9 lower labials

Diagnostic Features

- Long moderately slender snake with keeled scales and finger-shaped head
- Rudimentary teeth in mouth
- Distinctly visible apical pits
- Black interior to the mouth displayed as part of defence
- Several irregular V-shaped markings on nape of neck and head

Possible Confusion

In Arabia, the egg eater can easily be mistaken for the North East African saw-scaled viper, *Echis pyramidum,* or the Burton's carpet viper, *Echis coloratus*. Egg eaters are much more slender and have a series of forward-facing dark V-shapes on the nape of the neck. Saw-scaled vipers lack the V-shaped markings and have a pale interior to the mouth (seldom exposed during defence). Egg eaters have a black interior to the mouth, which is exposed during threat response.

Distribution

Most of sub-Saharan Africa to Ethiopia, Sudan and Somalia. Also recorded from Egypt and Morocco. In Arabia, it is known from south-western Saudi Arabia and western Yemen.

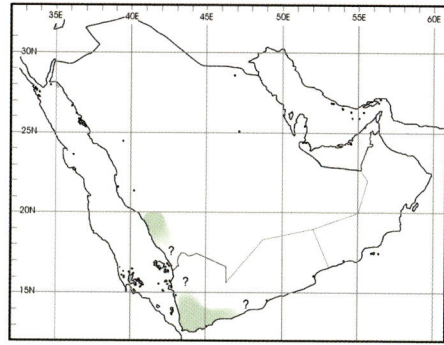

Natural History

Egg eaters are found in savannah, riverine forest, mountain grassland and rocky wadis. They usually shelter under rocks, in hollow logs and unused termite mounds.

They feed exclusively on bird eggs. As this diet is seasonal, they have the ability to fast for several months of the year.

Nocturnal, egg eaters are primarily terrestrial but will climb trees in search of eggs. Once an egg has been located, the snake will surround it with a coil of its body to keep it in place, and then slowly ease the jaws and head over it, engulfing it in one piece. Small projections on the spine are employed to effectively saw open the egg. Once the continuity of its form is broken, the egg collapses into a boat-shape. The contents are then swallowed and the collapsed shell is regurgitated.

Egg eaters mimic saw-scaled vipers, both in defensive behaviour and pattern. When threatened, the egg eater will coil into the typical horseshoe posture and rub its rough keeled scales together to create a rasping noise. It inflates the body and flattens out the head to create a more viper-like display. It will also strike out, but seldom makes contact, as its teeth are rudimentary and greatly reduced.

Above & top: *Rhombic egg eaters from an unknown locality in East Africa.*

Crowned Dwarf Snake

Eirenis coronella coronella   *(Schlegel, 1837)*

 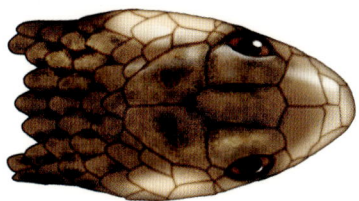

Description

Crowned dwarf snakes average about 25-30 cm in total length. The head is wider than the body and is slightly distinct. The eyes are moderate with round pupils and dark irises. The body is moderately stout, has smooth dorsal scales and is fairly round in section. The tail is indistinct and constitutes about 18-20% of the total length.

The dorsal surface is usually pale brown or grey with darker bands consisting of stippling or spots. A thick brown, crescent-shaped collar may meet the ventral surface or even pass through it on the throat. The underside is yellowish white with round brown spots.

Details

Mid-body scale rows: 15, smooth with visible apical pits
Anal: Divided
Subcaudals: 37-52, divided
Ventrals: 123-163
Head scales: 7 upper labials with 3rd and 4th entering the eye; 1 preocular; 1 postocular; anterior chin shields large in contact with 3 or 4 lower labials; posterior chin shields small and separated by a scale

Diagnostic Features

- Large crescent-shaped collar on nape of neck
- Anterior and posterior chin shields separated by a scale
- Apical pits visible on scales

Possible Confusion

Not likely to be confused for any other species in its range within the Arabian Peninsula.

Distribution

This species is widely distributed throughout the Middle East. Within the region covered by this book, it is known from the extreme north-east of Saudi Arabia along the Arabian Gulf shore and the northern border with Kuwait and Iraq.

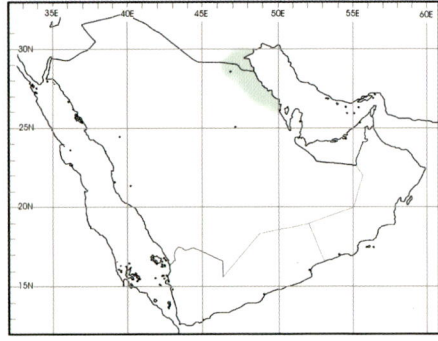

Natural History

Dwarf snakes inhabit a variety of habitats from arid alluvial plains to a more temperate Mediterranean environment.

   Diurnal or crepuscular, they feed on small lizards and possibly soft-bodied invertebrates. They are often found in agricultural land and other man-made habitats.

Previous, above & below: *Crowned dwarf snakes from Jordan.*

Fennell's Dwarf Snake

Eirenis coronella fennelli   *Arnold, 1982*

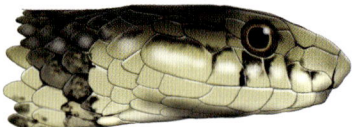 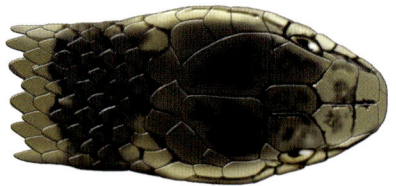

Description

Fennell's dwarf snakes reach around 31 cm in total length. The head is proportionately large but not distinct from the body. The snout is moderate and tapers to a squared off appearance. The head scales are slightly contoured and smooth. The eyes are moderately large and distinct with brownish irises and round pupils. The body is moderately stout and roundish in section. The body can be flattened slightly at will. The tail is indistinct and constitutes 19-21% of the total length.

The base colour is tan or greyish brown with dark, roughly rectangular or rhomboid dorsal blotches, either as saddles or bisected with the halves alternating each other in a checkerboard fashion. A series of lateral blotches continues this pattern on the flanks, which become progressively lighter towards the ventrum. The top of the head is dark grey/brown and a blotched stripe extends from either eye to the lip. A thick dark collar on the nape fades towards the throat.

Details

Mid-body scale rows: 17 anteriorly, 15 over most of the body – smooth, matte
Anal: Divided
Subcaudals: 59, divided
Ventrals: 131-154
Head scales: Rostral wider than high with convex posterior margin; internasals broader than long; prefrontals longer than distance from snout; small shield-shaped frontal twice as long as wide and shorter than distance from snout; supraoculars longer than frontal and wider than frontal posteriorly; nasal twice as long as high; small loreal; 1 preocular; 2 postoculars; 7 upper labials, 3rd and 4th in contact with eye; small mental; 8 lower labials, anterior chin shields large in contact with first 4 lower labials

Diagnostic Features

- Small robust snake with checkerboard pattern and collar on neck
- Head not easily distinguished from the neck

Possible Confusion

Unlikely to be easily confused with other species within its range. Colouration has a passing resemblance to hooded malpolons, *Malpolon moilensis* and leaf-nosed snakes, *Lytorhynchus diadema*. Both of these snakes are much more slender than dwarf snakes and have a very distinct neck.

Distribution

This subspecies is known from the northern and central Asir Mountains in Saudi Arabia.

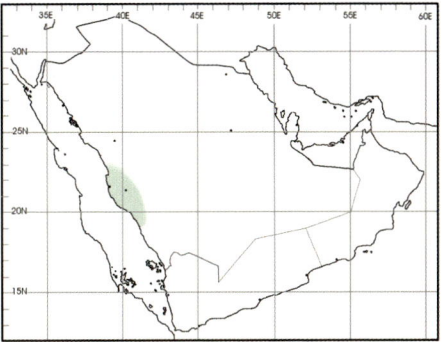

Natural History

This rare snake is only known from a few specimens and very little is known about its natural history. It has been found mostly at altitudes above 200 m in areas with good precipitation.

Arabian House Snake

Lamprophis fuliginosus arabicus   *(Parker, 1930)*

Description

House snakes may exceptionally reach 100 cm or more but are more commonly 60-75 cm. The head is slender and roughly coffin-shaped and is distinct from the body. The eyes are quite large, with an elliptical pupil and gold/brown iris. The neck is thin and the body is moderately slender and oval in section, being slightly laterally compressed. The body scales are smooth and shiny. The ventral scales are well developed. The tail is indistinct and constitutes around 10-13% of the total length.

The colour of this snake is variable throughout its range. The base colour tends to be dark brown on the dorsal surface and pearly white on the ventral surface. A light stripe runs from just above the snout, through the eye and along the flank on either side. These lines fade within the first-third of the body and may break up to form an irregular pattern. A second stripe extends from behind the eye, terminating at the corner of the mouth. Young specimens are more distinctly marked, whereas older ones tend to only have patterns on the head, or none at all.

Details

Mid-body scale rows: 28-33
Ventrals: 186-228
Anal: Entire
Subcaudal: 45-71, divided
Head scales: 2 postoculars; 1+2 temporals (occasionally 1+3, 2+2 or 2+3); 8 upper labials with 4th and 5th entering orbit; 8-10 lower labials (usually 9)

Diagnostic Features

- Glossy dark brown snake with distinct coffin-shaped head and slit pupils
- May have pale stripes on the side of the head and the flanks

Possible Confusion

Uniform brownish wadi racers, *Platyceps rhodorachus,* and cat snakes, *Telescopus dhara* resemble house snakes. House snakes are easily distinguished from racers as they have an elliptical pupil, are much more stout and are almost never seen during the day. Racers have round pupils, are very slender and diurnal. Cat snakes have larger eyes and more flattened heads than house snakes, and are generally much more slender and laterally compressed. Even very drab cat snakes tend to have a faint pattern which is not present in Arabian house snakes.

Distribution

Known from a scattered distribution in south-western Yemen and probably up into the Asir Mountains too.

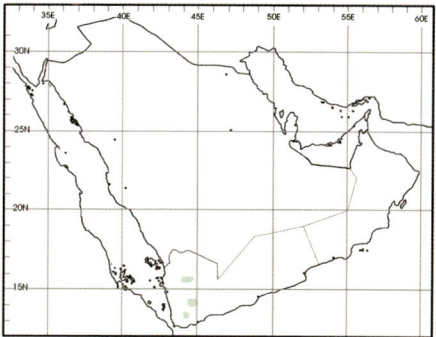

Natural History

House snakes occupy many habitats including grassland, acacia woodland, mountain slopes and riverine forest. They have been found mostly in mountain habitats in Arabia.

Opportunistic, house snakes will feed on most small vertebrates. Juveniles feed on geckos and sleeping lizards, while adults tend to show a preference for rodents. Prey is killed by constriction.

The house snake complex is nocturnal and actively forages for prey. Throughout their huge range in Africa, they are extremely useful in controlling rodents around homes and farmsteads. As the name implies, house snakes are willing to coexist with humans and will happily make a home of a barn, shed or other man-made structures.

Between 9 and 16 eggs are laid in late spring or summer. The incubation period is around 70-90 days. Hatchlings measure about 25 cm.

Above & below: House snakes from unknown localities.

Cape Wolf Snake

Lycophidion capense capense   *(Smith, 1831)*

Description

Wolf snakes reach a maximum length of around 60 cm in total length, but adults generally measure between 40 and 45 cm.

The head is relatively flat and coffin-shaped and covered in smooth glossy plates. The eyes are fairly small with elliptical pupils. The iris colour may be grey or bluish. The neck is moderate but easily distinguishable.

The body is neither thick nor thin and is vaguely triangular in section, although it can be flattened at will. The tail is distinct with a prominent hemipenal bulge in males.

Scales are smooth and very glossy. The tail constitutes about 10 or 11% of the total length (longer in males).

The dorsal surface is black, dark purple-brown, tan or olive grey. Each dorsal scale has a small white, grey or lavender spot on it. These spots get progressively larger towards the flanks. The ventral surface is white or pale grey (sometimes blackish).

Some specimens are uniform without any pale stippling. This is often the case with older specimens although many retain the patterning.

Details

Mid-body scale rows: 17
Anal: Entire
Subcaudals: 25-42, divided
Ventrals: 163-200
Head scales: Single nasal; small postnasal; internasals 1/2-2/3 length of prefrontals; frontal triangular; single preocular equal or larger than supraocular; temporals 1+2; 8 upper labials normally 3rd, 4th and 5th entering orbit; 8 lower labials (rarely 7), 1st, 4th or 5th in contact with chin shield

95

Species Identification Guide

Diagnostic Features

- Small stout dark snake with small eyes, elliptical pupils and distinct neck
- White speckling becoming more pronounced on flanks
- 17 dorsal scale rows
- 25-42 subcaudals
- Large maxillary teeth, first 7 increase in size posteriorly

Possible Confusion

Manser's racer, *Platyceps manseri* is a similar colour and size but has large eyes with round pupils and a much more slender body. Young burrowing asps, *Atractaspis microlepidota* may resemble wolf snakes, but have an indistinct neck, proportionately longer body and tiny eyes with a flat, spade-shaped head.

Distribution

In Arabia this species is known from one specimen allegedly collected in 1932 in south-western Yemen. It is unclear if this species is actually extant in the region. Elsewhere it is widespread throughout southern and eastern Africa.

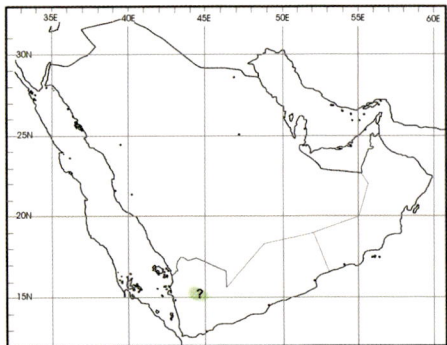

Natural History

In Africa, wolf snakes are most common in grassland and savannah, where they seek refuge underground or in unused termitaria. Nocturnal, they feed exclusively on smooth bodied scincoid lizards which are constricted before swallowing. Captive specimens refused all species of gecko and lacertids, but avidly consumed skinks of the genus *Mabuya* and *Acontias*. The large, recurved teeth give the snake its name.

Wolf snakes are inoffensive and seldom bite if handled.

A cape wolf snake from South Africa.

Crowned Leaf-nosed Snake

Lytorhynchus diadema   *(Dumeril, Bibron & Dumeril, 1854)*

Description

Leaf-nosed snakes may exceptionally reach 44 cm in total length but are more commonly around 30 cm.

The head is narrow and snout long with a well-developed rostral scale. The eyes are large with an elliptical pupil that does not extend as close to the edges of the iris as other snakes with vertical pupils. The proportionately large head is easily distinguished from the body by a thinner neck region.

The body is slender and rounded in section. Body scales are smooth and glossy. The tail is indistinct and constitutes between 17 and 19% of the total body length.

The colour and markings of this species are highly variable. Most commonly in Arabia, the base colour is tan or pinkish brown. A row of 13-18 chocolate-brown blotches cover the dorsal surface of the snake. Each blotch is edged in white or pink. The flanks may or may not be marked with longitudinal flecks. The ventral surface is white, cream or salmon pink. Another form has similar patterns but with a yellowish-brown base colour and brick-red blotches.

Details

Mid-body scale rows: 19
Anal: Divided
Subcaudals: 33-49
Ventrals: 152-195
Head scales: 1+2 or 2+3 temporals; 8 upper labials, 4th and 5th entering eye; 3 lower labials in contact with chin shields; posterior chin shields separated by 2 rows of scales

Diagnostic Features

- 152-195 ventrals
- 33-49 subcaudals
- Ovoid bars in series along back
- Small, moderately slender snake with large shield-like rostral scale

Possible Confusion

Gasperetti's leaf-nosed snake, *Lytorhynchus gasperettii* is similar in form but has an irregular vertebral stripe interspersed with pale oblong markings, unlike the dark blotches of *L. diadema*. Young hooded malpolons, *Malpolon moilensis* look similar to leaf-nosed snakes but have very large reddish eyes, round pupils and a beak-like face without the protruding shield.

Distribution

Widespread throughout the Arabian Peninsula. Absent from mountains and the interior sands of the Rub al-Khali.

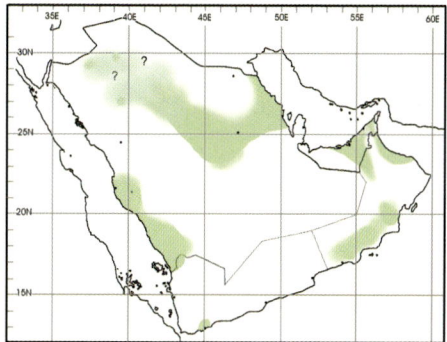

Natural History

This species occupies sandy desert, gravel plains and *sabkha* marshes. Nocturnal, they retreat to rodent burrows during the day. They feed exclusively on lizards. Captive specimens refused rodents, and several diurnal lizards, but accepted geckos of the genus *Bunopis, Stenodactylus* and *Pristurus*. Prey is killed by repetitive chewing with possible subduing action from oral secretions. The snake usually wraps around the prey animal. This is not constriction, but rather just a means of restraint. Aggressive if disturbed, leaf-nosed snakes hiss loudly and make mock strikes. Occasionally they will hide the head under a coil of the body.

Top: *A typical specimen of the leaf-nosed snake from Jordan.*

Above: *A darker specimen from Sharjah, UAE.*

Left: *An example of the rare 'Kennedyi' colour phase from Jordan.*

Gasperetti's Leaf-nosed Snake

Lytorhynchus gasperettii   *Leviton, 1977*

Description

Gasperetti's leaf-nosed snake probably attains a maximum length of around 40 cm. In form, they are similar to the common leaf-nosed snake with a proportionately larger head and shorter body. Mid-dorsal scales are keeled.

The background colour is grey or sandy brown. A series of 40 or so white oblongs run along the spine. These are interspersed with large brown diamond-shaped blotches that fuse around the white forming a more or less continual stripe. Another series of brown blotches run along either flank. The ventral surface is white. Each dorsal scale is edged in white, giving the snake a distinctly matte appearance. The point of a brown, forward-pointing arrow on top of the head terminates just between the eyes.

Details

Mid-body scale rows: 19 mid-dorsal scales keeled with apical pits visible
Anal: Divided
Subcaudals: 40-44, divided
Ventrals: 155-167
Head scales: 8 or 9 upper labials, 4th touching orbit; 3 lower labials in contact with anterior chin shields

Diagnostic Features

- Small snake with enlarged rostral scale and smooth dorsal scales, both keeled
- 33 mid-dorsal blotches joining to form rough stripe with small white oblongs

Species Identification Guide

Possible Confusion

The crowned leaf-nosed snake, *L. diadema* is similar but has a distinctly different pattern with 35 dark ovoid blotches. *L. diadema* has smooth dorsal scales throughout as opposed to the keeled mid-dorsal scales of *L. gasperettii*.

Distribution

Known from two localities in the Asir Mountains of Saudi Arabia.

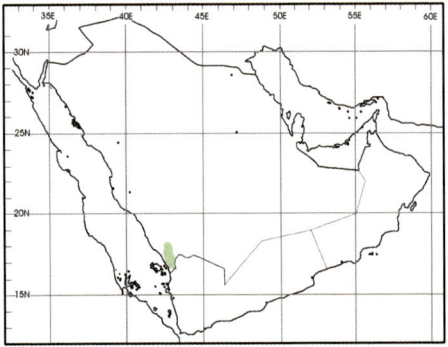

Natural History

Little is known of the ecology and private life of this snake. Presumably they are oviparous. They are nocturnal and probably feed on lizards.

False Cobra, Hooded Malpolon

Malpolon moilensis   *Reuss, 1834*

Description

Malpolons reach a maximum size of 189 cm (Libya) but adults of 70-80 cm are more common. The head is deep and pointed, and shield-shaped if viewed from above. The eyes are very large and reddish in colour with distinct round pupils.

The body is long, but muscular and thick. It is generally roundish in section but the snake can become extremely flat at will. The tail is slightly distinct and hemipenal bulges can be seen in males. Dorsal scales are large, smooth (but slightly grooved) and plate-like, often with interstitial skin showing in parts. The contour and pattern of the scales gives the snake a beaded appearance. The tail constitutes

around 17-20% of the total body length (longer in males).

The colour and pattern is fairly constant. The background is straw-coloured with alternating grey-brown blocks running the length of the vertebral region, giving a checkered appearance. The flanks have a further row of alternating grey-brown spots running the length of the body, smaller in size and wider spaced. The ventral surface is cream or white. A large dark brown or black blotch runs along the cheek to the angle of the jaw. Some specimens have a smaller dark patch directly behind the eye.

Details

Mid-body scale rows: 17
Anal: Divided
Subocular: 48-73, divided
Ventral: 159-176
Head scales: 2 postoculars; 2+2 or 2+4 temporals; 8 upper labials, 4th and 5th or 3rd and 4th entering the eye; 4 or 5 lower labials in contact with anterior chin shields

Species Identification Guide

Diagnostic Features

- Large snake that spreads a hood but faces danger with the back of the hood
- Large snake with pointed snout and huge eyes
- Dark spot on angle of jaw
- Large bead-like dorsal scales

Possible Confusion

Leaf-nosed snakes, *Lytorhynchus diadema* resemble baby malpolons at a glance, but have smaller eyes, a protruding rostral shield and lack the black spot on either side of the head. If a malpolon is approached, it will speed away whereas a leaf-nosed snake is relatively slow moving.

Distribution

Widespread throughout the Arabian Peninsula. Absent from the sand desert regions of the northern interior and Rub al-Khali, as well as mountainous regions. Elsewhere they are known from North and North East Africa, Jordan, Iraq and south-eastern Iran.

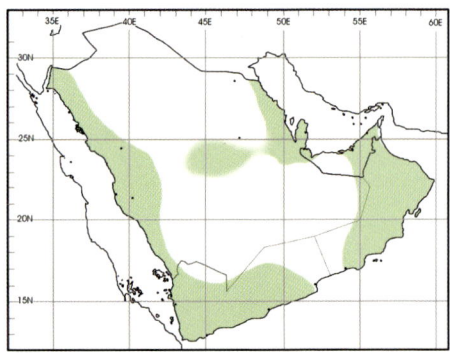

Natural History

This species occupies sandy desert, gravel plains and steppes, as well as foothills and coastal plains. They are diurnal and highly active foraging down rodent burrows and under litter. Rodents, fledgling birds and lizards such as *Acanthodactylus* and *Trapelis* are consumed. Malpolons have fangs situated roughly under the eye, and venom capable of subduing a rat in seconds. They are, however, considered to be harmless to humans. Symptoms of one bite (on the author) included mild local pain and limited swelling which subsided within 24 hours. Another bite (the author's sister) from a fairly large specimen that 'chewed' on the site for some time before releasing produced significant swelling that only subsided after a week. If molested, malpolons will escape at high speed. If cornered they will display a hood reminiscent of cobras, but generally face the attacker with the back of the hood.

Top: *A fairly dark hooded malpolon (Ra's al-Khaimah, UAE).*

Above: *Typical specimen showing threat response (Sharjah, UAE).*

Left: *A typical malpolon from Al Dhaid, UAE.*

Semi-ornate Snake

Meizodon semiornatus semiornatus   *(Peters, 1854)*

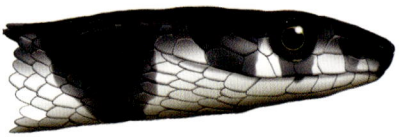 

Description

Semi-ornate snakes reach a maximum size of 65 cm but are more commonly found at around 45-50 cm. The head is distinct, slightly flattened and with a thinner neck region. The snout is moderate and tapers to a rounded rostral area. Head shields are flat and shiny. The eyes are moderately large with a dark grey iris and round pupil. The body is smooth, moderately slender and roundish in section, being very slightly laterally compressed. The slender tail can be distinguished at certain angles, and constitutes 24-30% of the total length.

The base colour is usually grey, olive brown or purple-grey. The anterior part of the body is banded in incomplete black bands or saddles. A thick dark band runs directly behind the eyes terminating at, or just below the lip. A second thick band occurs on the nape of the neck and terminates in points just before the ventral region. The ventral surface is uniform white, cream or grey. Older specimens fade significantly with some even becoming patternless.

Details

Mid-body scale rows: 21, smooth and shiny
Anal: Divided
Subcaudals: 73-93
Ventrals: 174-202
Head scales: Frontal is shorter than parietals and is as long as the distance from snout; loreal is longer than deep; 1 (occasionally 2) preoculars in contact with frontal; 2 postoculars (rarely 1); 8 upper labials, 5th and 6th in contact with eye; 9 or 10 lower labials, 1st and 5th in contact with anterior chin shields

Diagnostic Features

- Small diurnal grey snake with bars on front half of body
- Eyes placed half way between tip of the snout and back of parietals
- More than 21 scale rows

Possible Confusion

Racers of the genus *Platyceps* closely resemble semi-ornate snakes. All racers have less than 19 dorsal scale rows at mid-body and generally have eyes situated at a shorter distance from the tip of the snout than from the back of the parietals (ie, shorter snouts).

Distribution

Sub-tropical southern Africa, extending north to Ethiopia and Somalia. In Arabia it has allegedly been recorded in south-western Yemen.

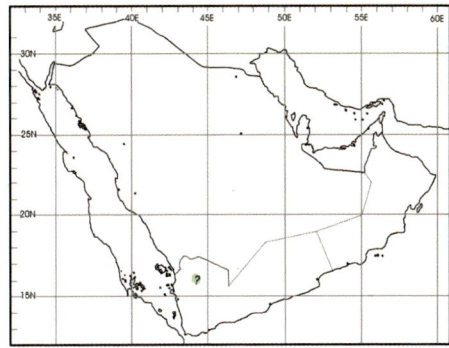

Natural History

Semi-ornate snakes are diurnal and normally associated with riverine habitats. They feed on frogs and various lizards and shelter in hollow trees and similar structure. Prey is probably killed by oral secretions. Although capable of climbing, most activity is terrestrial.

A typical semi-ornate snake from southern Africa.

Dice Snake

Natrix tessalata tessalata   *(Laurenti, 1768)*

Description

Dice snakes attain a maximum length in excess of a metre, but adults of 75–95 cm are more common. The head is roughly coffin-shaped and fairly deep. The snout is fairly squared off in cross section, whereas the rest of the head is rounded. The eyes are moderately small in adults and situated quite far forward, with pale irises and round pupils.

The head is easily distinguished from the body by a thinner neck region. The body is long but stocky and muscular and is more or less round in section, often with a muscular ridge on either side of the spine. The dorsal scales are keeled and the snake has an overall waxy appearance. The tail is slightly distinct from the body and constitutes about 18–20% of the total length.

Dice snakes are variable in colour. The background colour may be green, brown, olive, blackish or grey. Alternating rows of dark bars, blotches or rhomboid markings form a checkerboard effect on the back. Some specimens have complete bars along the back and some have no markings at all. Some specimens have a forward facing V-marking on the nape of the neck.

Details

Mid-body scale rows: 19, keeled except 2 outer rows
Ventrals: 160-197
Anal: Divided
Subcaudals: 48-86
Head scales: Rostral broader than deep; nasal semi-divided; internasals roughly triangular, as long as broad; frontal up to twice as long as broad, almost as long as the distance from snout; 2 or rarely 3 preoculars; subocular may or may not be present; 3 postoculars; 8 upper labials, 4th and 5th, or 5th and 6th in contact with eye; 4 or 5 lower labials in contact with anterior chin shields

Diagnostic Features

- Large, slender yet muscular colubrid snake with keeled scales
- Divided anal scale
- Generally found in the vicinity of permanent water

Possible Confusion

Young specimens could be mistaken for other small stout colubrids such as *Eirenis*. They differ from all similar looking snakes in that the dorsal scales are distinctly keeled. They are never found far from water.

Distribution

In Arabia, a single specimen was reported from western Yemen, although the species is extant in Jordan and the far north of Saudi Arabia. Elsewhere, it has a massive distribution from the Nile Delta, through most of the Mediterranean to southern and eastern Europe and western Asia.

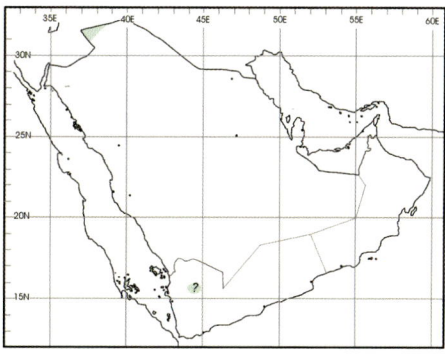

Natural History

Dice snakes are truly water dependent and lead an amphibious life. They are diurnal and often observed hunting or basking in streams. The diet consists of amphibians and fish, which are constricted. If disturbed, dice snakes often regurgitate, defecate and then sham death by coiling the body up while opening the mouth and even sticking the tongue out. They are unaggressive and completely harmless.

Up to 25 eggs are laid in summer, in organic debris or loose soil under stones or logs etc.

Above & below: A dice snake from Croatia.

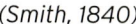

Spotted Bush Snake

Philothamnus semivariegatus semivariegatus   *(Smith, 1840)*

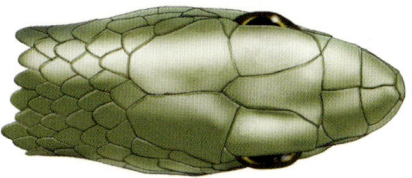

Description

Bush snakes attain a maximum length of about 95 cm, but adults are more commonly between 70 and 80 cm. The head is distinct and the eyes are very large. The pupils are round and edged in gold. The irises are dark brown, sometimes heavily flecked in gold. The snout is short and pointed. The neck is thin. The body is very slender and long with smooth, slightly overlapping dorsal scales. The ventral and subcaudal scales are keeled and possess lateral notches for purchase while climbing. The tail is very long and slender and constitutes about 32% of the total length.

African specimens come in a variety of regional colour morphs. Bush snakes suspected to be from Arabia are evidently olive with black variegations on the dorsum that fade out towards the rear of the body. The most common African morphs are green or olive grey with black variegations that fade towards the rear. The base colour may be consistent, or change to lighter colour on the posterior half. The ventral surface may be whitish, lime green or light brown, rarely bright yellow.

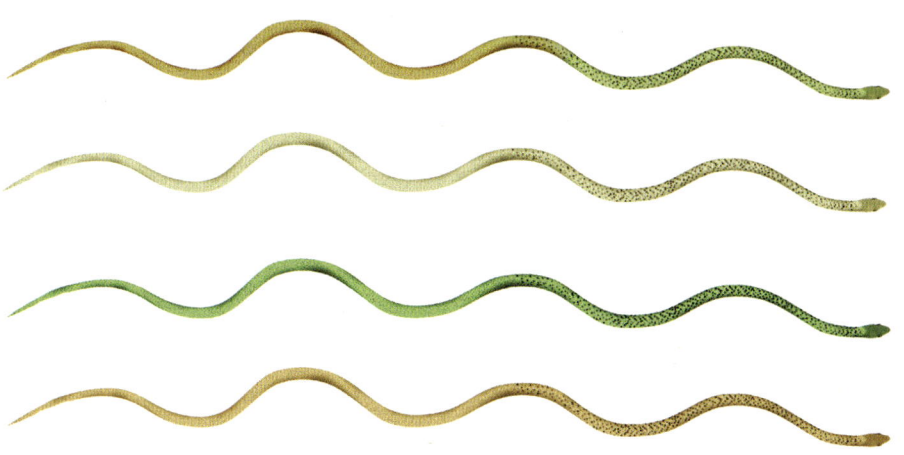

Species Identification Guide

Details

Mid-body scale rows: 15, smooth
Anal: Divided
Subcaudals: 122-166, divided
Ventrals: 175-204, keeled and notched laterally
Head scales: 2 postoculars; 8-12 upper labials usually with the 4th, 5th and 6th entering the eye; 9-12 lower labials

Diagnostic Features

- Only greenish barred snake in its range
- Keeled and notched subcaudal and ventral scales
- Inflates throat as a threat response, showing blue interstitial skin

Possible Confusion

Bush snakes are superficially similar to wadi racers, *Platyceps rhodorachus*. Indistinctly patterned specimens may be mistaken for sand snakes, *Psammophis schokari*. Bush snakes have laterally keeled ventral scales, and patterning consists of transverse rows of spots. Even dull sand snakes usually have longitudinal striping.

Distribution

In Arabia, it is known from a single specimen allegedly collected in western Yemen in 1932. Elsewhere, it occurs throughout sub-Saharan Africa in suitable habitat.

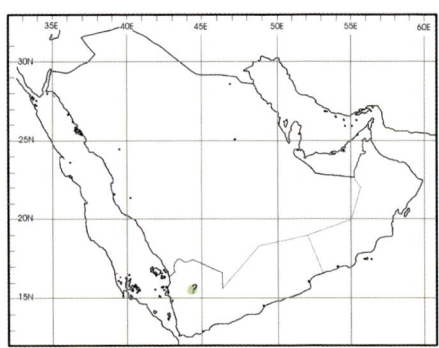

Natural History

Bush snakes inhabit savannah, riverine forest and most habitats with sufficient bush or tree cover.

They feed mostly on lizards such as geckos and young chameleons. Fledgling birds and frogs are also avidly consumed.

Bush snakes are active daytime predators often seen (in Africa) around eves of homes and in gardens. They are extremely fast and adept at spotting even slight movement made by such well-camouflaged prey as chameleons. Once seized, the prey is vigorously chewed upon after which it succumbs to the mildly toxic saliva.

Escape is the primary defence of the spotted bush snake. If the snake is restrained or cornered it will inflate the throat, displaying bright blue interstitial skin in contrast to the black and green of the scales. They will actively bite in such cases, but bites only result in a very mild itching that passes within a few minutes.

Bush snakes lay 3–12 elongated eggs in mid to late summer. Hatchlings are about 25 cm long.

Spotted bush snakes are harmless.

Above & top: *Common colour morphs of the spotted bush snake from southern Africa.*

Afro-Asian Sand Snake

Psammophis schokari schokari   *(Forskal, 1775)*

Description

Sand snakes may exceptionally reach 1.5 m but adult lengths of 70–90 cm are more common, with 1 metre specimens being quite rare.

The head is long, narrow and shaped like a deep coffin, tapering gradually to a narrow snout. The eyes are large and light in colour with a round pupil.

The head is easily distinguished by a very thin neck region. The body is very long and slender, and is slightly compressed in section. The long tail is virtually indistinguishable from the body as the taper is very slight. It constitutes around 24–35% of the total length. Scales are smooth without contour, but the snake is matte.

The colour and pattern of sand snakes is variable. Two common forms exist. The first consists of a tan, or putty-coloured background with a pale tan-dotted line, consisting of small suture-like marks, running along the spine. A broad, dark-edged pale stripe runs between dorsum and flank down either side with a chocolate-coloured stripe of similar width below just reaching the ventral scales. The ventral surface is white or cream with heavy blackish or brown pigment forming a stripe along the ventral scales. Some specimens have a yellowish ventral stripe edged in black.

The second form is dark brown with a thin, black edged, whitish dorsal stripe, a yellowish stripe above the flanks and white stripe entering the ventral scales. Uniform brown specimens have also been found. The head has a complex pattern on top and a thick dark stripe extending on either side from the snout, through the eye and into the patterns of the general body.

Details

Mid-body scale rows: 17-19, smooth
Subcaudals: 95-149, divided
Anal: Divided
Ventrals: 162-194
Head scales: Rostral wider than high; 2-4 shields surround the nostril; internasals shorter than prefrontals; one preocular, sometimes divided, in contact with the frontal; 2 rarely 3 postoculars; 8-10 upper labials with 3rd, 4th and 5th in contact with preocular and 5th and 6th in contact with eye; 5 or 6 lower labials in contact with anterior chin shields

Diagnostic Features

- Only slender snake with longitudinal stripes and big distinct eyes
- Grooved fangs below the rear of the eye
- Large eyes and very slender body capable of extreme speed

Possible Confusion

As very few Arabian snakes have vertebral stripes, it is unlikely that this snake will be easily confused with others. Variable racers, *Platyceps variabilis* occasionally have a vertebral stripe, but are heavier set and unlikely to exceed 40 cm. Young sand snakes have very slender bodies and huge eyes.

Distribution

Common and widely distributed throughout the Arabian Peninsula. Absent from the Empty Quarter and the north-west Hizaj Mountains. This species extends its distribution with development of urban green belts. Elsewhere it is known from north-eastern Africa to western Asia.

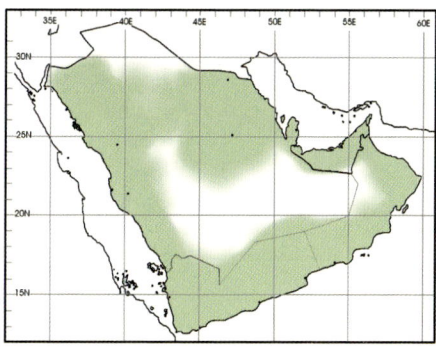

Natural History

Sand snakes occupy most habitats except high mountains and unvegetated desert. They are adept at thriving near human habitation and are common in parks and greenbelts.

Afro-Asian sand snakes are opportunistic feeders that will predate on most small vertebrates. Young birds, rodents, lizards of any description and bats are all consumed.

Sand snakes rely on their acute vision to locate the movement of prey items. They are among the fastest snakes in Arabia and can easily outstrip all but the most agile of prey.

Up to 9 small oblong eggs are laid in July or August and the hatchlings emerge after around 50-60 days of incubation (temperature dependent). Hatchlings measure around 30 cm and are exceptionally thin. Sand snakes have venom which is highly effective against prey. They seldom bite in defence even if restrained. One bite produces mild itching reminiscent of a mosquito bite, for about 20 minutes.

Top: *A typical sand snake from Sharjah, UAE.*

Above: *An unusually coloured sand snake from Sana'a, Yemen.*

Palestine Black-headed Snake

Rhynchocalamus melanocephalus   *(Jan, 1862)*

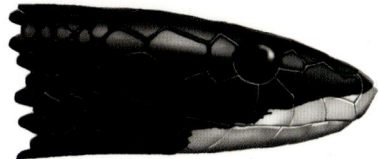 

Description

Black-headed snakes average around 40-48 cm in total length. The head is slightly distinct from the body. The snout is moderate, with the distance from the snout to eye being slightly longer than the distance from the eye to the back tip of the parietal scales. The eyes are moderate but indistinct due to the black colouration of the eyes and head alike.

Pupils are round. The body is long and slender, and round in section. The tail is indistinct and constitutes around 16-17% of the total length.

The base dorsal colour is tan, reddish brown or pinkish. The ventral surface is white, pinkish or slightly yellowish. The top of the head and neck are black with the rostral scale and upper lip being white.

Details

Mid-body scale rows: 15, smooth, moderately shiny
Anal: Divided
Subcaudals: 53-68
Ventrals: 181-229
Head scales: Entire nasal; internasals nearly as long as prefrontals; frontal longer than distance from snout; may or may not have small square loreal; one preocular and one postocular; 7 upper labials, 3rd and 4th in contact with eye; 3 or 4 lower labials in contact with chin shields; small posterior chin shields

Diagnostic Features

- Small, slender, light brown snake with pitch-black head
- If viewed from above, rostral scale is as long as distance from frontal
- Less than 70 subcaudals

Species Identification Guide

Possible Confusion

Black-headed snakes are unlikely to be mistaken for any other snakes within their Arabian range.

Distribution

Egypt, Lebanon, Palestine, western Syria, Jordan and possibly the extreme north of Saudi Arabia.

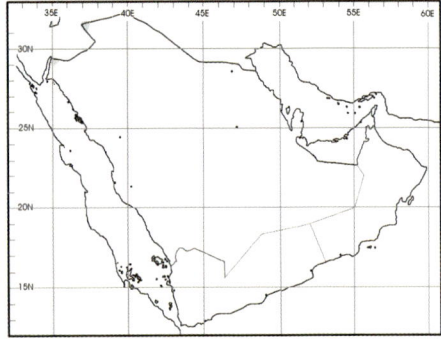

Natural History

Black-headed snakes occupy rocky and agricultural areas. They can be found in abandoned buildings, rubbish dumps and nearby human habitation. They are predominantly nocturnal and feed on a variety of invertebrates such as ant larvae, crickets, centipedes and locusts. They may also feed on small geckos and other lizards. This species is harmless to man.

A specimen of the Palestine black-headed snake from Jordan.

Aden Black-headed Snake

Rhynchocalamus arabicus   *Schmidt, 1933*

Description

The only known specimen of the Aden black-headed snake measured 27.8 cm in total length, with a tail measuring 4.9 cm. The head is slightly distinct from the body, being marginally wider than the neck region. Head scales lack much contour and are very shiny. The eyes are moderate but indistinct being dark on the black background of the snake's head. The body is slender and round in section. The tail is indistinct at 17.6% of the total length of the body.

The entire body is black with faint, pale outlines on the dorsal scales. The ventral surface is purple-black.

Details

Mid-body scale rows: 15, smooth and shiny
Neck scale rows: 21 up to the first ventral, then dropping to 15
Anal: Divided
Subcaudals: 81, divided, except for last 5 which are entire
Ventrals: 240, angulate
Head scales: Rostral offset from surrounding scales extending nearly half way to frontal; internasal suture half as long as that of prefrontals; frontal wide, and as long as distance from snout; supraoculars are narrow anteriorly; parietals large; nasal undivided; 1 preocular; 1 postocular; 4 or 5 upper labials; 8 lower labials, in contact behind the mentals; posterior chin shields indistinct from gulars

Diagnostic Features

- Small, slender, black snake with slightly distinct head
- 21 dorsal scale rows on neck becoming 15 after 1st ventral
- Broad frontal scale

Possible Confusion

Only likely to be confused with racers of the *Platyceps variabilis* complex. Black-headed snakes have a large rostral that extends quite far towards the eye. They also have 21 scale rows at the neck region and very narrow supraoculars.

Distribution

Known from a single specimen collected near Aden.

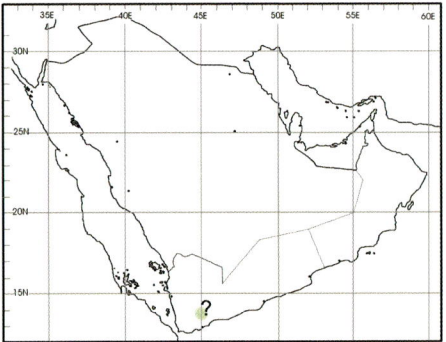

Natural History

Nothing is known about the behaviour of this snake. Due to its close relation to the Palestine black-headed snake, it might be assumed to be an insectivore and nocturnal.

Clifford's Diadem Snake

Spalerosophis diadema cliffordi   *Schlegel, 1837*

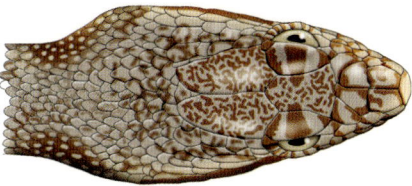

Description

Diadem snakes may exceptionally reach 1.3 m (Egypt) but adults of 90-100 cm are more common in Arabia.

The head is moderate, coffin-shaped and fairly deep. It tapers from the angle of the jaw to a fairly narrow snout. The eyes are moderate with pale irises and round pupils.The head is easily distinguished from the body by a thinner, albeit muscular neck region. The body is thick and long, being slightly compressed and square in section. The tail is indistinct and constitutes around 17-19% of the total length (longer in males).

Variable in colour, most commonly the base colour is grey, tan or reddish brown with a series of brown ovoid blotches running along the spine. These may or may not be edged in white. A further row of smaller blotches runs along each flank in alternate sequence to the spinal blotches. A third row of similar sized, or slightly smaller spots run below these and enters the ventral surface. On some specimens the spinal blotches are merged in parts and are only distinct from each other by thin, irregular pale bars. Scales may have pale-edged scales.

Details

Mid-body scale rows: 25-29, lightly keeled
Ventrals: 210-248, slightly angulate laterally
Anal: Entire
Subcaudals: 64-81 , divided
Head scales: Rostral as deep as broad or broader; prefrontals broken up into several shields; frontal as long as wide, as long as, or slightly shorter than the distance from snout; 3-5 loreals; 2-4 preoculars, upper usually in contact with frontal; 3-4 postoculars; labials separated from eye by suboculars; 10-13 lower labials; 5 lower labials in contact with anterior chin shields

Species Identification Guide

Diagnostic Features

- Large grey snake with moderate eyes, dark blotches and lightly keeled scales
- Head plates irregular
- Sub-ocular scales between eye and upper labials

Possible Confusion

Babies might be mistaken for leaf-nosed snakes, *Lytorhynchus diadema*. Leaf-nosed snakes have vertical elliptical pupils and an enlarged, shield-like rostral scale. Adults are unlikely to be mistaken for any other species.

Distribution

Widely distributed in suitable habitat throughout the region. Absent from the sandy desert of the Rub al-Khali, Northern Interior, and the plains of the Jiddat al-Harasis. Elsewhere, it is known from North Africa, through the Middle East, to Iran.

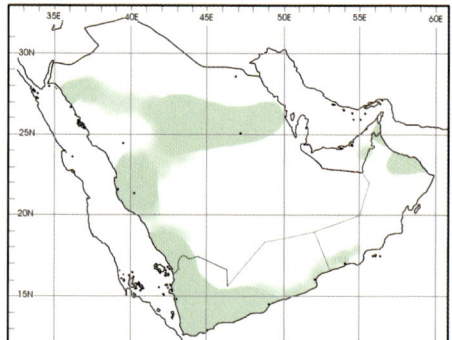

Natural History

Diadem rat snakes inhabit gravel plains, savannah, foothills and mountain plateaus. They are generally crepuscular by habit but have been known to move at any time of the day or night. Rodents constitute the bulk of the adult diet with juveniles feeding primarily on small lizards. Prey is constricted before being swallowed. This is a truly useful snake to humans and where it occurs in large densities (specifically North Africa) it has a marked impact on rodent populations. Diadem snakes lay eggs in early summer and hatchlings emerge after an incubation of 70–90 days. Hatchlings measure around 30 cm and are proportionately slender with a large head. Diadem snakes are quick to escape but are highly aggressive if cornered or restrained and large specimens can produce painful bites. They are harmless.

Above & below: *An adult diadem snake from Masafi, UAE.*

Arabian Cat Snake

Telescopus dhara   *(Forskal, 1775)*

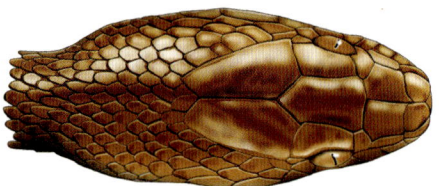

Description

Cat snakes reach a maximum of 95 cm but are more commonly 60-70 cm in total length as adults. The head is slightly flattened (although it can be further flattened as a threat response) and covered in smooth glossy shields. The eyes are large with pale irises and an elliptical pupil.

The broad head is easily distinguished from the body by a thin neck. The body is slender and slightly laterally compressed, being sub-triangular in section. The tail is indistinct and constitutes around 12-14% of the total length. There is little visible difference between males and females.

Highly variable in colour, cat snakes are most commonly tan with heavy brown, roughly rectangular blotches along the spine. Two further rows of roundish blotches run along the flanks. Some specimens have a similar pattern with a pinkish-brown base colour and bright orange spots. Specimens devoid of all but the faintest pattern are also fairly common, specifically in northern Yemen and southern Saudi Arabia. These tend to be uniform brown with dark-edged scales and a pale impression of the pattern. The ventral surface is normally cream or yellowish, as are the upper labials.

Details

Mid-body scale rows: 19-21, smooth with visible apical pits
Ventrals: 235-274
Anal: Entire
Subcaudals: 66-72, divided
Head scales: Rostral much broader than high; internasals wider than long; prefrontals 1/2 the length of frontal; frontal longer than the distance from snout; parietals longer than frontals,

longer than wide; occasional small shields behind parietals; nasal single plate with cleft behind nostril; loreal twice as long as deep; 1 preocular; 2 postoculars; 9-10 upper labials, usually 3rd, 4th and 5th entering eye; 3-5 lower labials in contact with chin shields; anterior chin shields longer than posterior

Diagnostic Features

- Broad, viper-like head with cat-like eyes and smooth slender body
- Sub-triangular in cross section
- Small fangs in line with the back of the eyes

Possible Confusion

Brown coloured wadi racers, *Platyceps rhodorachus* resemble cat snakes in colour and may be confusing if the snake is moving. Cat snakes have a larger, more distinct head and elliptical pupils. House snakes, *Lamprophis fuliginosus arabicus* have a similar colour to the brown phase of the cat snake, but are shinier and have a longer, less flattened head, much smaller eyes, as well as a body that is round in cross section, much stouter and more glossy.

Distribution

They occur around most of the coastal mountain fringe of Arabia, the plains of the Jiddat al-Harasis, as well as the mountains and outcrops of the Northern Interior.

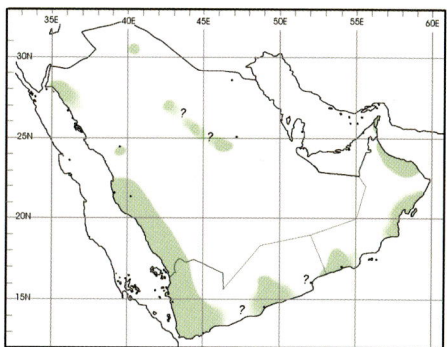

Natural History

Cat snakes occupy arid rocky areas. Excellent climbers, they will often climb trees and rock faces in search of prey. Prey includes bats, small birds and lizards (especially chameleons). Captive specimens took sparrow nestlings and geckos but refused rodents.

When threatened, cat snakes assume a striking position and flatten the head out to appear more imposing. They will not hesitate to strike and tend to hold on after defensive bites. The venom is of no concern to man and generally causes a mildly numbing sensation and a small amount of localized swelling at the immediate site of the bite.

Around 7-11 eggs are laid in early summer and incubate for around 65 days. Hatchlings measure around 25 cm and are more strikingly marked than the adults.

Above: *A patternless brown specimen of the cat snake from Ta'izz, Yemen.*

Below: *A bright orange specimen (caught in Sharjah, but was probably transported in date palms from northern Oman).*

Revoil's Short Snake

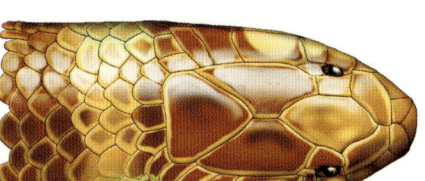

Brachyophis revoili revoili   *Moscquard, 1888*

Description

Revoil's short snakes attain an assumed maximum total length of around 30 cm. The specimen reportedly collected in Yemen measured a total length of 22.5 cm. The head is flattened and spade-shaped. The eyes are tiny with elliptical pupils.

The head is indistinct and is the same width at the neck and body.

The body is thick, short and slightly flattened in section. The tail is short and distinct, constituting around 5–8% of the total length. Dorsal scales are smooth and shiny.

Revoil's short snake is tan or cream-coloured with thick brick-red bars running the length of the body. These fade towards the ventral surface. The ventral scales are also yellowish cream with darker edges.

Details

Mid-body scale rows: 15, smooth
Anal: Entire
Subcaudals: 8-13
Ventrals: 104-118, well developed and broad
Head scales: Large rostral; large hexagonal frontal, longer than broad; prefrontals longer than internasals, large pointed occipital shaped in a triangle or pentagon; 7 upper labials, 3rd and 4th in contact with the eye, 5th and 6th in contact with parietals; 2 large chin shields separated by 2 rows of small scales

Diagnostic Features

- Small, fat, whitish snake with red-brown bars and tiny eyes
- Hexagonal chin shields

Possible Confusion

Unlikely to be confused with any other species. Although the head is similar to burrowing asps, *Atractaspis microlepidota*, the extreme colour difference and the short, stocky body of the Revoil's short snake is obvious.

Distribution

Known from the southern coast of Somalia. One specimen was recorded from western Yemen in 1932. It is possible, but very surprising considering the limited African distribution of this species, a considerable distance from Yemen.

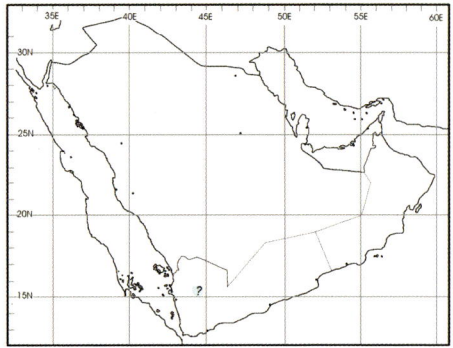

Natural History

Very little is known of the natural history of the short snakes. They are fossorial and probably dependent on substrate moisture for survival. Due to several physiological similarities to other members of the *Atractaspididae*, it may be surmised that they feed on fossorial lizards or other snakes. The composition of the venom of this species is completely unknown.

Previous, above & below: A preserved Revoil's short snake from Somalia.

Small-scaled Burrowing Asp Complex

Atractaspis microlepidota   *Gunther, 1866*
Including:
Anderson's Burrowing Asp
A. m. andersoni   *Boulenger, 1905*
Ein Geddi's Burrowing Asp
A. m. engaddensis   *Haas, 1950*

 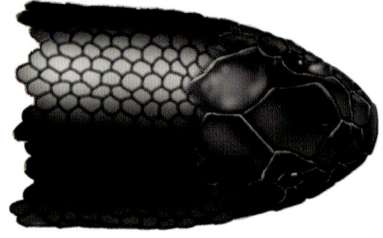

Description

Burrowing asps may exceptionally reach 90 cm, but are generally 60-70 cm as adults. The head is flattened, spade-shaped and indistinct from the body and neck. The eyes are small and indistinct with round pupils. Although fairly long and slender, adults become quite stocky. The body scales are smooth and glossy with little or no overlap. The tail is indistinct, constitutes around 7-8% of the total body length and terminates in a small spike. A pair or cluster of long fangs are attached to the maxillary bones and lie perpendicular to the jaw.

Although generally black in colour, dark brown specimens have been recorded. Just prior to sloughing, some specimens may appear bluish grey.

Details

Atractaspis microlepidota andersoni

Mid-body scale rows: 23-25
Ventrals: 218-254
Anal: Entire
Subcaudal: 23-40, entire
Head scales: 1 preocular, normally divided; 1 postocular; temporals resemble large dorsals; 6 or 7 upper labials, 4th or 3rd and 4th entering the eye; 3 or 4 lower labials in contact with chin shields

Atractaspis microlepidota engaddensis

Mid-body scale rows: 27-29
Ventrals: 264-282
Anal: Entire
Subcaudal: 31-40, entire
Head scales: 1 preocular, normally divided on the lower half; 1 postocular; temporals resemble large dorsals; 6 or 7 upper labials, 4th or 3rd and 4th entering the eye; 3 or 4 lower labials in contact with chin shields

Diagnostic Features

- Shiny black snake with shovel-shaped head, tiny eyes and no visible neck
- Small spike on end of tail
- A cluster of large, back-facing fangs on the maxillary bone, occasionally protruding from the sides of the mouth

Possible Confusion

Young specimens of the desert black snake, *Walterinnesia aegyptia* may resemble burrowing asps but have a large head that is easily distinguished by the thinner neck, and much larger eyes placed laterally. Burrowing asps have extremely flat, rounded heads.
Anderson's burrowing asp is virtually identical to the northern Ein Geddi's burrowing asp. Apart from geographical location, scale differences need to be analyzed in order to differentiate them.
A. m. andersoni: Generally occurs below 18°N; has a fully divided nasal scale; 23-25 mid-body scale rows; 216-254 ventral scales and 27-33 subcaudals.
A. m. engaddensis: Generally occurs above 18°N; the lower half of the nasal scale is divided; 27-29 mid-body scale rows; 264-282 ventrals and 32-40 subcaudals.

Distribution

From the Asir Mountains of Saudi Arabia, the Yemen highlands, through to Dhofar. They probably have a scattered distribution in the Hadramaut. *A. m. andersoni* is marked with green on the map. *A. m. engaddensis* is marked with blue.

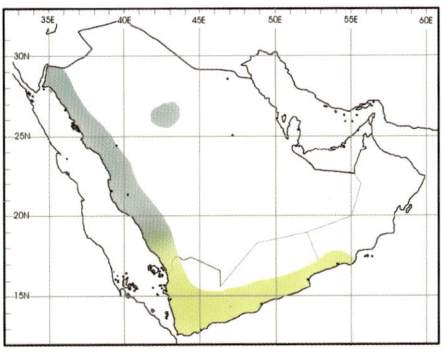

Natural History

Being predominantly fossorial, burrowing asps are seldom seen on the surface. Rarely they can be seen at the entrances to rodent burrows, rocky clefts and caves during wet weather. Generally, they utilize networks of rodent and invertebrate burrows to navigate and only surface if flooded or moving to a new location. They are non-aggressive and sluggish if disturbed during the day, but can put on a surprising turn of speed at night. If provoked, they will often hide the head beneath a coil of the body, or arch the neck and back with the nose pushed into the ground if disturbed. Although reluctant, burrowing asps will strike out if molested. They do so in a characteristic jerky, sideways motion.

They are opportunistic feeders, preying on snakes, lizards, amphibians and rodents.

The long recurved fangs are a perfect adaptation to killing prey in a cramped burrow. The mouth need not be completely open for envenomation to take place. This adaptation should be kept in mind, as there is virtually no safe way to handle this snake!

Note: The Ein Geddi burrowing asp is treated as a subspecies of the small-scaled burrowing asp here. It may well be a separate species under the greater *A. microlepidota* complex.

Atractaspis m. cf. engaddensis *from near Jeddah in western Saudi Arabia.*

Above & below: Atractaspis microlepidota andersoni *from Sana'a, Yemen.*

Arabian Cobra

Naja haje arabica   *Scortecci, 1832*

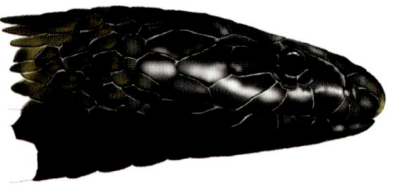

Description

Arabian cobras may exceptionally reach 190 cm or more, but are more commonly 120-150 cm. The head is covered in large smooth shields. The eyes are moderate with round pupils and dark irises. The head is distinguishable from the body by a thinner neck. The neck can flatten out forming a characteristic hood if the snake is threatened. The body is long and fairly slender, although older specimens tend to be quite stocky. Body scales are smooth and large, arranged in distinctive diagonal transverse rows. Only the three scale rows closest to the ventrals do not follow this pattern. The ventrals are well developed. The tail constitutes around 20% of the total length and is not easily distinguishable from the body. Males have longer tails with a fairly prominent hemipenal bulge. Short fixed fangs are present in front of the mouth.

Cobras are found in several very striking colour morphs. The head and tail are most commonly black or dark brown. The rest of the dorsal surface may be reddish brown, dark brown, bright yellow or orange. Some orange specimens have a yellow head and no black at all on the body. The ventral scales may be black, dark purple, brown or cream. On most specimens the throat area is black. Hatchlings may be a dull version of the adult colouration or grey with black extremities.

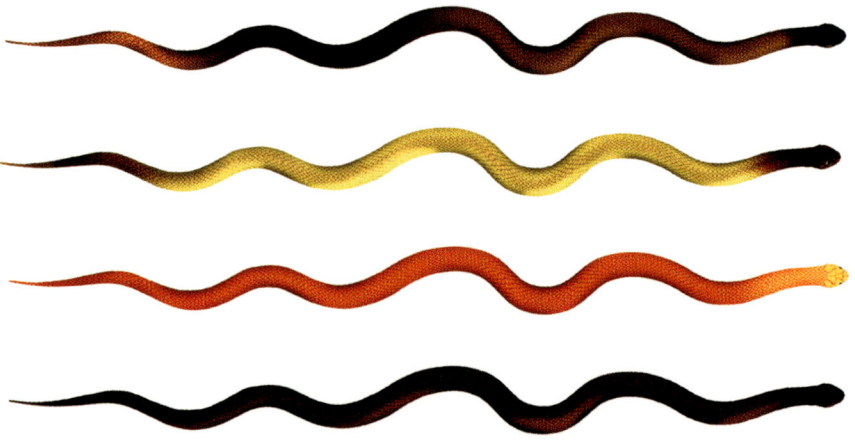

Details

Mid body scale rows: 19-21 rows
Neck rows: 21-23
Ventrals: 202-226
Anal: Entire
Subcaudals: 62-80, divided and undivided together
Head scales: 2 or 3 postoculars; 2 or 3 suboculars (separating eye from labials); 1+2 or 1+3 temporals; 7 or 8 upper labials (3rd enlarged, 6th or 7th in contact with lower postocular); 4 lower labials in contact with chin shield

Diagnostic Features

- Large, smooth but matte snake that spreads a hood if cornered
- Randomly arranged combination of divided and entire subcaudals
- Dorsal scales make distinctive diagonal rows along the body

Possible Confusion

Baby specimens could be mistaken for racers of the genus *Platyceps*, some of which share a similar colour, and are also active during the day. Cobras are more stoutly built and babies have a disproportionately large head, when compared to the petite proportions of racers.

Distribution

From the vicinity of Taif, in western Saudi Arabia, south to Aden, then east, scattered through the Hadramaut, to Dhofar.

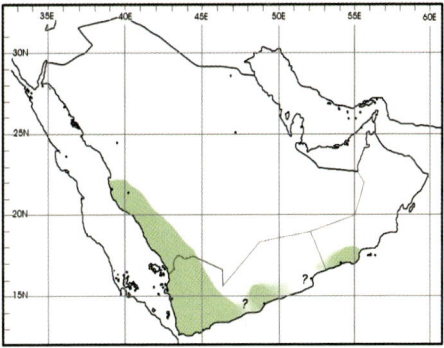

Natural History

They inhabit mountain highlands, generally 1,500 m or more above sea level. They have a preference for rocky, well-vegetated terrain and are relatively water dependent.

Opportunistic, cobras will eat most vertebrates. Toads *(Bufo dhufarensis)* are favoured, probably due to availability and ease of capture. Rodents, birds, eggs, lizards and other snakes are readily consumed. Large agile snakes, Arabian cobras are elusive and seldom seen. They are diurnal, being most active in the cool of early morning and late evening. They are active hunters and energetically shovel and probe about between stones and in loose soil in search of prey. Eyesight plays an important role in hunting and they are capable of actively pursuing even such fast animals as rats with success, although a more common strategy would be cornering rodents within their burrows.

When disturbed, they are usually extremely fast to retreat, but if cornered, will raise the head and up to a third of the body off the ground and confront the source of danger. A wide hood is formed by spreading out ribs in the neck region, making the snake look larger and more imposing. Arabian cobras possess a very potent neurotoxin. This venom is life-threatening and fast acting!

Previous, above & below: *Various colour morphs of the Arabian cobra from Taif, Saudi Arabia. The yellowish specimen below is a fairly common variant.*

Desert Black Snake, Black Desert Cobra

Walterinnesia aegyptia   *Lataste, 1887*

Description

Desert black snakes may exceptionally reach 1.4 m but adults usually measure around 90-100 cm. The head is broad and covered in large glossy head shields. The eyes are small and dark, with round pupils. The rostral scale is thickened and well developed. The head is distinct from the body although the neck region is thick.

The body is thick, elongate and sub-triangular in section. Dorsal scales are smooth on the anterior portion of the body, becoming faintly keeled towards the posterior. The snake has a very glossy appearance. The tail is slightly distinct and constitutes around 11% of the total length.

They are completely black in colour with a bright blue iridescence when viewed in the sunlight. The ventral surface is also black and is even more iridescent.

Details

Mid-body scale rows: 21-25, smooth anteriorly becoming faintly keeled posteriorly, glossy
Ventrals: 180-200
Anal: Divided
Subcaudal: 40-53, up to 13 entire, remainder divided
Head scales: Rostral broader than deep; internasals as long as prefrontals; frontal longer than wide, as long as the distance from rostral; posterior nasal in contact with single preocular; preocular more than twice as long as deep; 2 postoculars; 1 subocular; 7 upper labials, 3rd and 4th entering eye; 4 lower labials in contact with anterior chin shields; anterior chin shields longer than posterior

Diagnostic Features

- Large shiny blue/black snake with enlarged rostral scale and thick body
- Dorsal scales faintly keeled towards the rear of the body
- Short, stout pair of fangs at the front of the mouth

Possible Confusion

Burrowing asps, *Atractaspis microlepidota* resemble young desert black snakes up to a point. These have rounded, spade-shaped heads and tiny eyes. The body is much longer and thinner, and the head is not distinguishable from the body.

Wolf snakes look a little like baby desert black snakes but have a longer head and thinner neck region. They appear to have mutually exclusive ranges.

Distribution

Absent from central and south-eastern Arabia, they have a large, if fragmented range throughout the north and east of the Peninsula. Elsewhere, they are known from North Africa, through the Middle East to Iran.

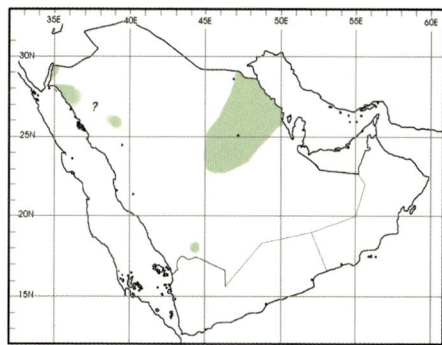

Natural History

Desert black snakes inhabit arid hilly terrain, gravel plains and scrubland. They are nocturnal and, at least in part, fossorial. Prey consists of lizards (particularly members of the genus *Uromastyx*) and rodents, which are usually cornered down holes. If disturbed, the snake will assume a striking position and hiss very loudly as a deterrent. Only prolonged disturbance or restraint would result in a bite.

Short fixed fangs, situated in front of the mouth deliver a potent neurotoxin. This snake has been responsible for human fatality and bites should be treated promptly.

Above & below: *A typical desert black snake from Jordan.*

Stokes' Sea Snake

Astrotia stokesii   *(Gray, 1846)*

Description

Stokes' sea snakes reach a maximum length of around 1.6 m, females being larger than males. The head is large and blunt and the neck region thick and indistinct. The snout tapers to a blunt point from the eyes and is as long as the distance from the eyes to the back of the head. Head shields are slightly contoured, smooth and shiny. The eyes are small and dark with a round pupil. The body is thick and almost rectangular in section anteriorly, being slightly laterally compressed. It becomes more compressed and rounded towards the posterior. The tail is flat and paddle-like.

Variable in colour, the base colour may be straw-yellow, whitish, grey or brown. 24-38 dark bands run the length of the body and are usually complete. Some specimens have thin lines between the banding, giving the snake a 'tiger-stripe' appearance. Some older specimens have dorsal bars and lateral blotches or spots.

Details

Mid-body scale rows: 45-63, keeled, spine-like or tipped with a dentoid protrusion
Neck scale rows: 35-47, keeled
Ventrals: 226-286, entire anteriorly, becoming broken up and cryptic within the front-third of the snake; ventrals have dentate tips
Head scales: 1 preocular and 2 postoculars; 8-10 upper labials, 2nd and sometimes 3rd in contact with prefrontal, 4th, 5th and 6th enter eye; 10-12 lower labials

Diagnostic Features

- Extremely robust sea snake with large head and rough scales
- 226 or more ventrals starting off entire and becoming broken up after a few rows
- Dentoid or serrated edges to ventral scales

141

Possible Confusion

Short sea snakes, *Lapemis curtus* have similar body proportions and rough scales. They generally have entire ventral scales, only occasionally breaking up towards the rear and spine-like protrusions on the flanks. Stokes' sea snakes have ventrals that invariably break up in the anterior third and have serrated or dentate margins on the ventrals.

Distribution

Known from Pakistan and India, Stokes' sea snake would represent a vagrant species in Arabian waters.

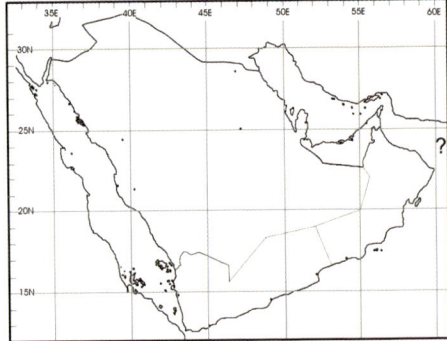

Natural History

Very little is known of the natural history of this snake. It occurs in rocky and coral reefs, as well as over sandy substrate, always in coastal waters. Goboid and other slender-bodied fish are consumed.

A banded specimen from South East Asia.

Beaked Sea Snake

Enhydrina schistosa   *(Daudin, 1803)*

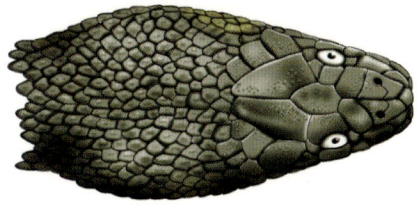

Description

Beaked sea snakes may reach 150 cm, but average between 110 cm and 130 cm. The head is blunt and rounded, covered in armour-like shields adorned with prominent tubercles. The snout is shaped like a beak. This is more prominent in juveniles. The eyes are gold with a round pupil. The head is slightly distinct. The bottom jaw is deep and prominent. The body is robust and laterally compressed, more so towards the rear of the body. The body scales are keeled. The flat, oar-like tail constitutes about 12% of the total length.

They are generally bluish grey or olive on the dorsal surface. The dorsal colour turns abruptly to white about half way down the flanks. About 40 black or olive bands run the length of the dorsum, terminating at the junction of the dorsal and ventral colours. Some adult specimens lack any banding.

Details

Mid-body scale rows: 49-69, overlapping, keeled
Anal: Entire, only slightly larger than dorsal scales
Ventrals: 230-354, reduced but easily visible
Head scales: 1 preocular; 1 postocular; 7-9 upper labials with 3rd and 4th, or 4th entering eye; elongated narrow mental scales

Diagnostic Features

- Upward pointing eyes
- Long dagger-shaped mental scales
- Beak-shaped snout

Possible Confusion

Short sea snakes, *Lapemis curtus*; Ornate sea snakes, *Hydrophis ornatus* and viperine sea snakes, *Praescutata viperina* all resemble beaked sea snakes. Beaked sea snakes can easily be identified by its upward pointing eyes and beak-shaped snout. The other three have eyes that point outward. The mental scale of the beaked sea snake is extremely long and thin compared to the others.

Distribution

Gulf of Oman and probably the Arabian Gulf. Elsewhere, it is known throughout South East Asia as far south as northern Australia.

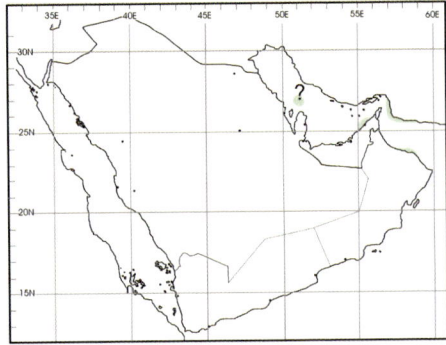

Natural History

Although found in reefs, beaked sea snakes prefer open shallow water with a sandy or muddy substrate. They are known to enter estuarine areas and lagoons.

Most small fish will be considered, but gobies (particularly shrimp gobies) and eels feature strongly in the diet, probably due to easy capture.

Venomous, beaked sea snakes will willingly bite if handled and are responsible for more snakebite (mostly South East Asia) than any other sea snake. Bites by *E. schistosa* in Arabian waters are virtually unheard of. They are non-aggressive if left alone.

A typical banded specimen of the beaked sea snake from Malaysia.

Annulated Sea Snake

Hydrophis cyanocinctus   *Daudin, 1803*

Description

Annulated sea snakes may exceptionally reach more than 2 m but are more commonly between 1.5 and 1.7 m. There is a slight distinction between the body and the head. The body is cylindrical and narrow towards the front becoming more laterally compressed and deep towards the rear. *H. cyanocinctus* is a long, slender snake. Ventral scales are keeled or are adorned with 2 or 3 tubercles. The ventrals are reduced, but distinct, being about twice the width of the dorsals. The tail is distinct and paddle-like, and constitutes around 8-10% of the total length.

Juveniles are distinctly marked with a yellowish base colour and bold black bands. The top of the head is black with a yellow horseshoe-shaped marking running through the eyes and down either side of the head.

Adults are variable. Mostly they are a faded version of the juveniles, with a silvery grey, whitish or pale yellow base colour. The bands are usually darkest on the dorsal surface, fading, as well as becoming narrower, as they reach the ventrals. Some adults have half bands or no bands at all.

Details

Mid-body scale rows: 33-48, imbricate with central keel
Anal: Enlarged
Ventrals: 280-397, enlarged, twice as large as dorsals anteriorly
Head scales: 7 or 8 upper labial with 2nd in contact with prefrontal; 1 preocular; 2 postoculars; 2 superposed anterior temporals

Diagnostic Features

- 50-75 dark bars fading towards the flanks separated by interspaces half as wide
- Long, very slender body
- Small eye placed high above mouth

Species Identification Guide

Possible Confusion

Arabian Gulf sea snakes, *H. lapemoides* and yellow sea snakes, *H. spiralis* resemble this species. Arabian Gulf sea snakes are shorter and stouter than annulated sea snakes. Juveniles look more similar to each other than the adults. Yellow sea snakes have much thinner bands on the body than annulated sea snakes.

Distribution

Throughout the Arabian Gulf and the Gulf of Oman. Elsewhere they are found throughout South East Asia to the Philippines.

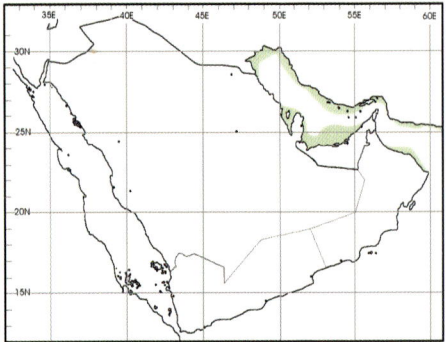

Natural History

Normally they are found in shallow coastal waters, over sandy substrate. They feed mostly on smooth bodied fish such as gobies and eels, possibly cephalopods as well.

Annulated sea snakes are abundant in the Arabian Gulf. They are often seen basking on the surface by recreational boaters, as well as being taken as by-catch by fishermen. Juveniles are quite often found stranded on the Gulf shores and may represent a risk to small children playing on the beach (there are, however, no reported cases of casualty sustained in this manner).

This species has caused human fatality, and will bite if restrained. They are not aggressive however and will tolerate much provoking.

Annulated sea snakes possess a potent myotoxin. Bites from this species have caused human fatality. Bites are rare and invariably happen to people handling the snakes.

Antivenom is effective against the venom of this species.

Above & below: *A neonate annulated sea snake from Ajman, UAE.*

Arabian Gulf Sea Snake

Hydrophis lapemoides   *(Gray, 1849)*

Description

Arabian Gulf sea snakes can reach over a metre, but adults of 80-90 cm are more common. The head is fairly large and distinct. The body scales are hexagonal, keeled, and as long as broad. Towards the rear, the scales are more extremely keeled and are wider. In the case of adult males, the posterior scales may have spine-like tubercles instead of keels. The body is neither thick nor thin and is laterally compressed. In adults, a deep keel develops along the posterior half of the body. The tail is paddle-shaped and constitutes around 8% of the total length.

Juveniles are white or pale yellow with striking black bands. The head is black with a prominent white horseshoe marking on top.

Adults usually have a grey or faded yellow base colour with greenish, or grey, bands. These bands fade towards the ventral surface and may be completely absent in old specimens.

Details

Mid-body scale rows: 40-51
Ventrals: 300-404
Head scales: 1 preocular; 2 postoculars; cunate scales at oral margin after 2nd or 3rd lower labial; 8 upper labials, 2nd in contact with prefrontal, 3rd and 4th (sometimes 5th) entering eye; 8-11 maxillary teeth behind fangs

Diagnostic Features

- 8-11 maxillary teeth behind fangs
- Cunate scales after 2nd or 3rd lower labial
- 40-51 mid-body scale rows
- 33-45 dark bands with interspace two times wider

Possible Confusion

Ornate sea snakes, *Hydrophis ornatus* and annulated sea snakes, *Hydrophis cyanocinctus* resemble *H. lapemoides*. Ornate sea snakes differ in having bands that terminate in a sharp point and lack cunates on the oral margin. Annulated sea snakes are similar in colour, but are much longer and thinner than Arabian Gulf sea snakes (the young of these two species are more similar than adults, if coiled up).

Distribution

Throughout the Arabian Gulf and the Gulf of Oman. Elsewhere they extend east to Sri Lanka and possibly further into South East Asia. Two specimens were reportedly captured off the coast of Penang.

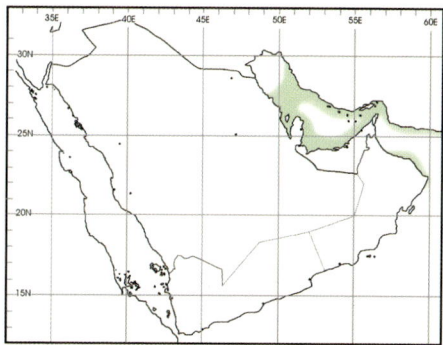

Natural History

This is a shallow-water species mostly found over open sandy substrates. They are occasionally found close to quite rough shore breaks in water less than three metres deep. They feed on most fish when available but will probably feed primarily on eels, goboids and flatfish, due to easier capture. In captivity, they have accepted a wide range of fish.

These are among the more commonly seen snakes in the Arabian Gulf and the Gulf of Oman. Elsewhere in their range, they are considered to be very rare. Within the region, they are usually observed during the day resting on the surface.

They are very often found washed up on the beach. Juveniles get caught in currents and boat-injured adults are not an uncommon sight. They are not aggressive, but still possess a potent myotoxic venom.

Above: *A neonate Arabian Gulf sea snake from Umm al-Qaiwain, UAE.*

Top & centre: *Adults from the shores of the Eastern Province, Saudi Arabia.*

Ornate Sea Snake

Hydrophis ornatus   *(Gray, 1842)*

Description

Ornate sea snakes may exceptionally reach 1 m, but are more commonly 80-90 cm. The head is large and defined. The body is neither slender nor thick and is compressed towards the rear. Older specimens tend to become more stocky. The tail is wide and paddle-shaped and constitutes between 9 and 12% of the total length.

Juveniles are distinctly marked with a yellowish background colour and thick black bands. The adults are olive green, brown or dark yellow, becoming progressively paler towards the belly. Thick black, dark brown or grey bands taper to a point just above the ventrals. The head is yellowish below and olive above, with or without a fragmented yellow horseshoe pattern.

Details

Mid-body scale rows: 33-55, keeled
Anal: Small, entire
Ventrals: 209-312
Head scales: Small scales between lower labials; 2 or 3 postoculars; 7 or 8 upper labials with 2nd in contact with prefrontals

Species Identification Guide

Diagnostic Features

- Distance between eyes is 1/2 or more than 1/2 the distance from snout to parietals
- Large distinct head
- Bands become distinctly ovoid or triangular in adults

Possible Confusion

Short sea snakes, *Lapemis curtus* and Arabian Gulf sea snakes, *Hydrophis lapemoides* resemble this species. Short sea snakes have proportionately thicker bodies and have very roughly keeled scales; more so than the ornate sea snake. The Arabian Gulf sea snake has a smaller, blunter head and bands that fade towards the ventral surface, rather than ending in a point.

Distribution

Throughout the Arabian Gulf and the Gulf of Oman, east to China and south, as far as northern Australia.

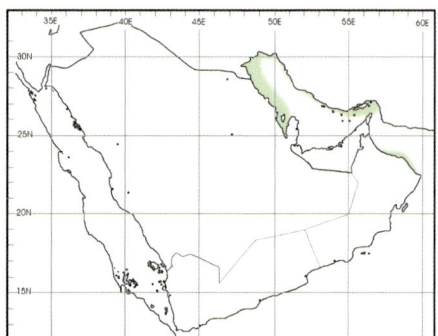

Natural History

Ornate sea snakes usually occupy coastal areas. They are most common in shallow, warm coastal waters over coral reef, sandy or muddy substrate. Several fish species are preyed upon, including many free-swimming varieties.

Very little is known about the life history of this snake.

Ornate sea snakes are locally quite rare. They are found occasionally basking in the sun on the surface, but are more commonly seen at night, just below the surface. The fact that they include certain free-swimming species of fish in their diet indicates that they probably prey on sleeping fish among corals etc at night.

Ornate sea snakes have a potent myotoxin. Fatalities have occurred as a result of the bite of this species.

An adult ornate sea snake from Malaysia.

Yellow Sea Snake

Hydrophis spiralis spiralis   *(Shaw, 1802)*

Description

Yellow sea snakes may exceptionally reach 2.7 m, but are more commonly 1.6-1.9 m. The head is moderate and indistinct and the body long and slender. The dorsal scales are roughly hexagonal, longer than broad and generally smooth, or with a small tubercle present. The ventrals are slightly larger than the body scales. The tail is distinct, deep and constitutes about 7 or 8% of the total length.

The dorsal colour is yellow, mustard or brown, becoming pale yellow or white on the flanks. About 30-60 narrow dark bands run the length of the body and tail. These bands may or may not be complete. In older specimens the bands may fade with a remnant of the original band running down either side. The tail often has irregular black blotching and the tip is usually black.

Details

Mid-body scale rows: 29-39
Ventrals: 282-373
Head scales: 6-8 upper labials with the 3rd and 4th, or 4th and 5th entering the eye; 1 preocular and 1 or 2 postoculars; 4 lower labials in contact with sublinguals

Diagnostic Features

- Long slender sea snake regularly reaching over 2 metres
- Normally less than 50 dark bands on the body (excluding tail)
- Bands are thin with wider interspaces, usually complete, retained as adults

Possible Confusion

Annulated sea snake, *Hydrophis cyanocinctus* are quite similar in appearance. Annulated sea snakes have much thicker bands on the body that tend to only remain distinct dorsally in adults, forming wide, incomplete bands.

Distribution

Throughout the Arabian Gulf and the Gulf of Oman, east to South East Asia as far as the Malay Archipelago.

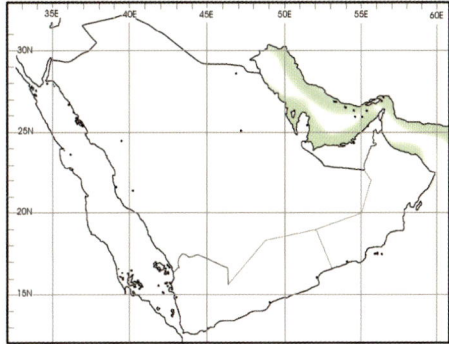

Natural History

Yellow sea snakes are generally found in shallow waters over coral reefs and sandy substrate. They feed heavily on eels and other slender, hole-dwelling fish. Very little is known of the natural history of this snake. They are occasionally seen close to shore, basking at the surface on calm days. Yellow sea snakes are the largest of all sea snakes.

Yellow sea snakes have a potent myotoxin. Bites from this snake have caused human fatality. Bites are rare however, and the snakes are not aggressive.

Above & below, left: *An adult from Khor Kalba, UAE.*

Below, right: *A 220 cm specimen from Dubai, UAE (boat collision).*

Short Sea Snake
Lapemis curtus   *(Shaw, 1802)*

Description

Short sea snakes may exceptionally reach 1 m, but average around 80 cm as adults. The head is large, blunt and is indistinct from the body. The head shields are robust and armour-like. The eyes are small with a round pupil. The body is thick and laterally compressed towards the rear. Ventral scales are greatly reduced and often break up towards the tail. Body scales are hexagonal, each with a single sharp keel in the centre. The keels closest to the dorsum are smallest. In mature males, these keels take the form of spines on the lower flanks. The paddle-like tail constitutes around 9% of the total body length.

Juveniles generally have a yellow base colour, a black head and incomplete black bands running the length of the body. A yellow stripe joins the two eyes and extends from the eyes along either side of the head. Adults are more variable. The base colour may be yellow, tan or pinkish, with black, brown or light grey bands. The tail tends to be darker. The yellow head pattern may or may not be present.

Details

Mid-body scale rows: Males: 30-39; females: 36-45, keeled
Neck scale rows: Males: 28-31; females: 31-35, keeled
Ventrals: 140-219
Preanals: Enlarged

Diagnostic Features

- Ventral scales barely wider than dorsals and becoming irregular towards rear
- Blunt, bulldog-like snout and long spine-like protrusions on the flanks of adults
- Less than 59 scale rows

Possible Confusion

Beaked sea snakes, *Enhydrina schistosa,* ornate sea snakes, *Hydrophis ornatus* and viperine sea snakes, *Praescutata viperina* resemble short sea snakes at a glance. Short sea snakes have a proportionately thicker, shorter body than other sea snakes. Older males are easily identified by the spine-like scales on the flanks.

Distribution

Throughout the southern Arabian Gulf, the Gulf of Oman, south-east to India. Short sea snakes are replaced in the south and east by the Hardwick's sea snake, *L. hardwickii.*

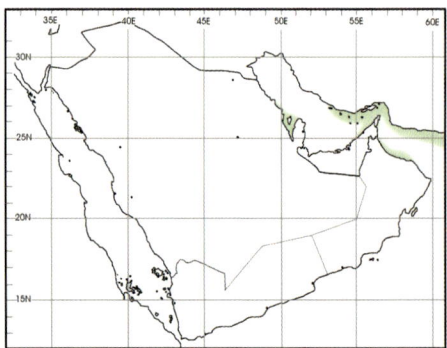

Natural History

Their behaviour and private life are largely unknown. Short sea snakes show a preference to shallow, murky waters, often near, or in river mouths and lagoons.

Gobies and eels feature strongly in their diet, but many species of fish are taken when available. Cephalopods such as cuttlefish and squid are also taken.

Although non-aggressive, they will readily bite if restrained or otherwise molested and have caused human fatalities. They possess a potent myotoxin.

An adult male specimen of the short sea snake from Malaysia. Note the spinose scales on the flanks.

Small-headed Sea Snake

Microcephalophis gracilis   *(Shaw, 1802)*

Description

Small-headed sea snakes may exceptionally reach 110 cm, but adults of around 85 cm are more common. This snake is very easily identified by its tiny head and deep body. The front-third of the body is shallow and slightly laterally compressed. It becomes extremely compressed and very deep towards the rear, where the body in cross section resembles that of many pelagic fish. The body scales are hexagonal and wider than long. The scales on the rear of the body have two or three tubercles, one behind the other. These are more prominent towards the ventral surface.

The ventrals are slightly wider than the body scales in front of the body, but become divided towards the rear. The eyes are moderate, dark in colour, and have round pupils. The tail is small, distinct and paddle-shaped, constituting around 8 or 9% of the total length.

Juveniles are blackish with a series of off-white bands. As the snake matures, the dorsal colour fades to grey, or bluish grey with a white belly. There may or may not be faded grey bands on the flanks. These terminate in a point. The head is black or dark grey.

Details

Mid-body scale rows: 29-36, tubercles or keels posteriorly
Neck scale rows: 17-19
Ventrals: 220-287, divided by furrow posteriorly
Anal: Slightly enlarged
Head scales: Diameter of orbit equal to distance from eye; rostral large extending onto upper snout; frontal small; 1 preocular; 1 postocular; single anterior temporal in front of large scale; 5 or 6 upper labials, 2nd in contact with prefrontal, 3rd and 4th in contact with eye; no small scales or oral margin between lower labials

Diagnostic Features

- Tiny head, narrow neck and narrow, deep posterior body
- Massive plate-like labial scales

Possible Confusion

Microcephalophis is unlikely to be mistaken for any other species of snake. There are no other marine snakes in the region with such a tiny head in comparison to the body size.

Distribution

Throughout the Arabian Gulf and Arabian Sea, although locally very rare. Elsewhere, they are known from India, east to China and much of South East Asia.

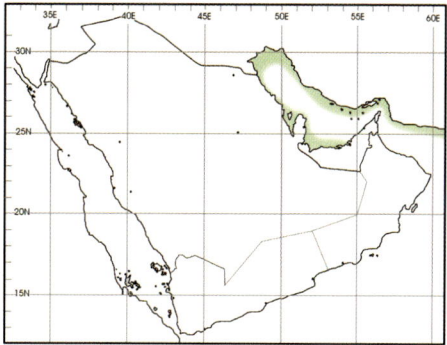

Natural History

Small-headed sea snakes are found in coastal waters, to a depth of around 50 m. They are generally found in clear waters with a sandy or coral substrate. These snakes can be found at more extreme depths than most sea snakes. They are often observed quite far offshore.

The tiny head of this snake enables it to probe into holes and crevasses, in search of gobies and other small slender fish. Out of water, it is completely helpless. Although the venom is highly toxic, the small mouth and placid nature of this snake ensure that snakebite is very uncommon.

An adult small-headed sea snake from Malaysia.

Pelagic Sea Snake

Pelamis platurus   *(Linnaeus, 1766)*

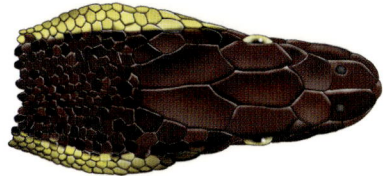

Description

Pelagic sea snakes may reach a total length of 1 m, but specimens of 70-80 cm are more common. The head is distinct from the body and the entire body is laterally compressed. The eyes are placed further back on the head than other sea snakes. The iris is pale with a round pupil. The body scales are as wide as long and are hexagonal in shape. 2 or 3 small tubercles exist on the lower rows of scales. This is more prominent in adults. The tail constitutes between 9 and 11% of the total body length.

The colour and pattern is variable. Generally the ventral surface and the flanks are yellow or pale brown. A thick black, grey or brown vertebral stripe runs the length of the body, becoming wavy posteriorly. The junction of the two colours is abrupt with no fading. The tail is spotted and blotched in black and whitish. Some specimens are mostly yellow with reduced black. Others lack the wavy pattern, but have a continuous straight vertebral stripe.

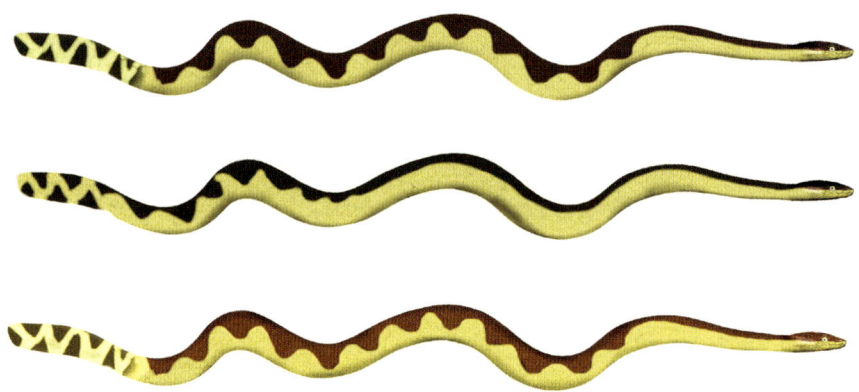

Details

Mid-body scale rows: 49-67, hexagonal
Ventrals: 264-406, divided by a medial ridge or broken up and indistinct
Anal: Moderately larger than dorsals
Head-scales: Frontal large, as long as the distance from snout; 1 or 2 preoculars; 2 or 3 postoculars; many small temporals; 7 or 8 upper labials, 2nd in contact with frontal, 4th and 5th separated from eye by suboculars; 10 or 11 lower labials; small chin shields; anterior sublinguals distinct, separated by small scales

Diagnostic Features

- Wavy dorsal stripe as opposed to banding
- Much longer, more slender head and snout than any other sea snake

Possible Confusion

This species is unlikely to be confused with other sea snakes. The deeply compressed body, narrow head and lack of banding are distinct.

Distribution

In Arabia, they are common throughout the Arabian Gulf and the Gulf of Oman.

The pelagic sea snake has the widest distribution of any snake. They occur from the west coast of the Americas, across the Pacific and Indian Ocean to Australia, South East Asia and on to east and southern Africa.

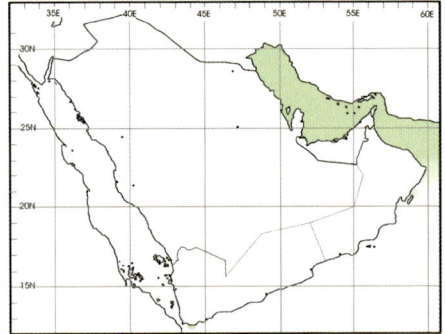

Natural History

Although found mostly in coastal waters, this snake frequents open seas. Attracted to slicks of flotsam such as organic debris or discarded material from ships.

This is a truly pelagic species. They spend most of their time on the surface, among floating debris where they lie in ambush for small shoaling fish. If surrounded by a shoal, a random, repetitive striking technique is employed. If a single fish is within range, a more precise strike is used.

Their distribution seems to be much at the mercy of ocean currents. Although they are powerful swimmers, their tendency to float around among flotsam can carry them very far indeed. It is this very behaviour that can also lead to hundreds, or even thousands of pelagic sea snakes congregating from time to time. Slicks of several hundred metres have been recorded off the shores of Pakistan and elsewhere.

The venom is apparently weaker than most sea snakes, but should be considered dangerous regardless. Bites are virtually unheard of as the snakes are very docile.

Above: *A typical pelagic sea snake from the Arabian Gulf, off the shore of Saudi Arabia.*

Below: *A pale specimen from Saudi Arabia.*

Viperine Sea Snake
Praescutata viperina   *(Schmidt, 1852)*

 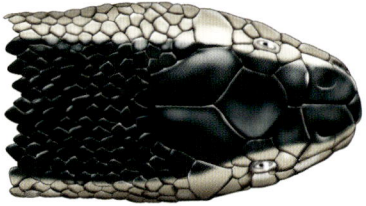

Description

Normally, viperine sea snakes are between 70 and 80 cm but may exceptionally reach 95 cm. The head is large, wide and distinct from the neck. The eyes are moderate, with a pale iris and round pupils. The body is relatively stout and laterally compressed. Adult males have spinose protrusion on the distal edge of the scales, and on the anterior ventral scales. The ventrals are as wide as the body on the front half of the body, becoming about twice as wide as the body scales towards the rear.

The paddle-like tail is distinct and constitutes around 9 or 10% of the total length.

The colour is variable. Generally the dorsal surface is grey, brownish or olive. A series of large dark spots runs the length of the spine. The ventral surface is pale. A more common colour variation in the Gulf is plain grey, or olive on the dorsum, and white on the ventral surface. The two colours meet on the flanks in a clear, straight line of demarcation. They may or may not have black bands.

Details

Mid-body scale rows: 27-50, keeled becoming spinose posteriorly in older males
Neck scale rows: 37-54, keeled
Ventrals: 226-291, very wide anteriorly, just under twice as wide as dorsals posteriorly
Anal: Enlarged
Head scales: Diameter equal to distance from mouth; nasal sub-triangular, as wide as long; prefrontals wider than long, not in contact with labials; frontal twice as wide as supraocular; 1 or 2 preoculars; 1 or 2 postoculars; 7-9 upper labials; temporals either single or 2 or 3 smaller scales; 4 lower labials in contact with sublinguals

Diagnostic Features

- Heavily built sea snake with very wide anterior ventrals
- Ventrals clearly visible along the whole length of the body

166

Possible Confusion

Beaked sea snakes, *Enhydrina schistosa* and short sea snakes, *Lapemis curtus* resemble viperine sea snakes up to a point. In both species, *Praescutata viperina* can be differentiated by the presence of very wide ventral scales and a proportionately wider head. *Lapemis curtus* is proportionately shorter and stouter and *Enhydrina schistosa* has upward-pointing eyes.

Distribution

Found throughout the Arabian Gulf and the Gulf of Oman in low numbers. Elsewhere they extend east to China and south to Malaysia.

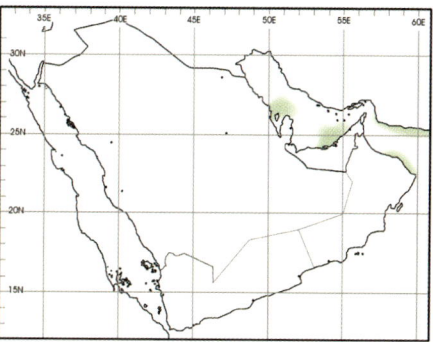

Natural History

Viperine sea snakes inhabit shallow warm coastal waters. They are known to enter lagoons, estuaries and creeks. Flatfish, goboid fish and eels are all consumed.

Very little is known about this snake. They give birth to small clutches (probably 3–5) of young in early summer.

They are apparently more mobile on land than most sea snakes and can crawl about (very laboured). Viperine sea snakes have a potent myotoxin and, although not aggressive, can deliver a life-threatening bite.

A viperine sea snake from Malaysia.

Puff Adder

Bitis arietans

(Merrem, 1820)

Description

In Arabia, adults may exceptionally reach 80 cm, but specimens of 60-70 cm are more common. Specimens from East Africa have been known to approach 2 m in total length.

The head is very wide and flat, and roughly triangular when viewed from above. There are no head shields present but rather small keeled scales. The eyes are small in adults but distinct and pale with elliptical vertical pupils. The head is very easily distinguished from the body by a thin neck region.

The body is short and very thick being rounded and flattened in cross section. The dorsal scales are heavily keeled giving the snake a very rough appearance. The ventral scales are very wide. The tail is short and constitutes 5-8% of the total body length.

Males have a thick tail that gradually tapers from the cloaca, whereas females have a short, thin and very distinct tail with a steep taper.

Colour may vary, but the pattern is more or less constant throughout the range. The base colour is tan or grey with darker patterning. A thick dark bar runs between the eyes. A similar bar runs from either eye to the lip. A diagonal bar runs from the rear of the eye to the angle of the jaw. A large, roughly rectangular marking covers most of the head. The body consists of a series of backward-pointing chevrons along the spine, edged with a dark smudge per chevron on the flanks. A row of pale, convex crescents enter these smudges with their points entering the ventral surface. The ventral scales are marked with irregular bars or blotches.

Details

Mid-body scale rows: 29-40, heavily keeled
Ventrals: 130-145, very wide and well developed
Anal: Entire
Subcaudals: 25-38, divided
Head scales: Small rostral; 8-11 inter-orbital scales; 12-16 circum-orbital scales; 3-4 series of scales between eye and upper labials; 2 or 3 series of scales between supranasals; 12-16 upper labials; 3-5 lower labials in contact with chin shields

Diagnostic Features

- Large viper wider than 5 cm with chevron pattern that hisses when disturbed
- Less than 35 subcaudals
- Nostrils directed slightly outwards

Possible Confusion

It is unlikely that adults will be confused with any other species due to the very fat body and wide head. Babies may be confused with other small vipers, but have a distinct chevron pattern and hiss when provoked. The broad, flat head with no raised tubercles or brow-ridge is unlike that of any other Arabian viper.

Distribution

Puff adders are found throughout Africa in suitable habitat. In Arabia they occupy the western mountains below 22°N through the Yemen highlands to Dhofar. Their occurrence within the Hadramaut complex is uncertain, although personal communication by the author with locals seems to indicate that it is extant in certain patches of habitat on the northern ridge, but rare.

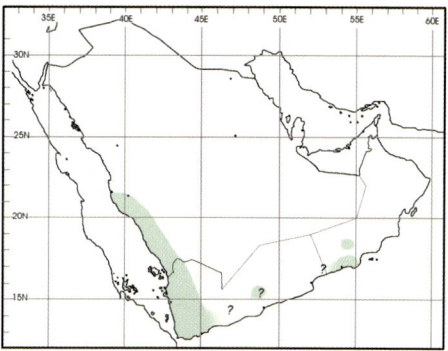

Natural History

Puff adders occupy savannah, foothills, rocky plains and grassland. They feed primarily on warm-blooded prey such as rodents and other small mammals or birds, as well as occasional reptile prey.

Puff adders are ambush predators, relying on their cryptic colouration to conceal their outline when lying among rocks or vegetation. The strike speed is among the fastest of any snake. Large prey is usually bitten and released after which the snake will follow the scent of the envenomated animal and swallow it at leisure.

If disturbed puff adders will assume a strike position with head raised above the ground and facing down. The body is inflated and deflated while the snake issues a loud hiss.

Puff adders are responsible for a high number of snakebite statistics in sub-Saharan Africa, where people are most commonly bitten on the foot or ankle after stepping on the snake. In Arabia they are responsible for less snakebite but still represent a potential hazard.

The potent cytotoxin causes swelling, discolouration and necrosis of the bite site. This may affect the entire limb. Amputations and other disabling effects are common with bites from large specimens of the puff adder.

Above & below: Typical puff adders from Taif and Asir Mountains, Saudi Arabia.

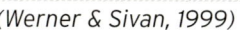

Hoofien's Horned Viper

Cerastes cerastes hoofieni   *(Werner & Sivan, 1999)*

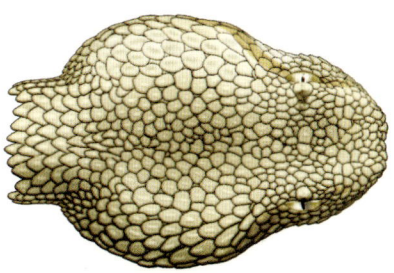

Description

Hoofien's horned vipers reach a maximum of around 80 cm in total length, but are more commonly around 50 cm as adults. The head is wide and triangular in form with a very thin neck area. The head is covered in small keeled scales. Some specimens have a stout horn above each eye composed of a single modified scale. Unlike the Arabian horned viper, the horn is generally more or less upright. Hornless specimens often don't have any trace of occipital tubercles. The eyes are moderate with an iris generally matching the body colour. The pupils are elliptical.

The body is stocky and short in proportion. Thinner specimens tend to be quite square in section. Well fed specimens are roundish and slightly flattened. The body scales are keeled giving the snake a rough appearance. The tail constitutes around 10-15% of the total length, is distinct and is visibly narrower in females.

As with the Arabian horned viper, the colour is variable in accordance to habitat and substrate colour. Grey, brown, tan or pinkish specimens have all been recorded. The pattern is fairly consistent and is comprised of darker rectangular or rhomboid bars running along the back, interspaced with lateral blotches or spots. The vertebral bars may break up towards the extremities to form a checkerboard pattern. Some very pale specimens are indistinctly marked.

Note: See the full-body illustrations of *C. gasperettii* for more colour variations. These two species share a number of identical colour morphs.

Species Identification Guide

Details

Mid-body scale rows: 29-39, strongly keeled with a rough appearance
Anal: Entire
Subcaudals: 23-45, paired
Ventrals: 150-167
Head scales: 11-15 supralabials, separated from eye by 4-5 scales; more than 14 interorbitals; supra-ocular horn consisting of a single scale may or may not be present and is generally shorter, stouter and more vertical than *C. gasperettii*

Diagnostic Features

- If horned, the horns are generally solid and upright
- 129-137 ventral scales
- More than 14 interorbitals

Possible Confusion

This species is sympatric with Arabian horned vipers, *Cerastes gasperettii* in parts of southern Saudi Arabia and Yemen. At a glance they are identical and almost impossible to tell apart. The primary difference is in the number of ventral scales. *C. cerastes* has 129-137 ventral scales, whereas *C. gasperettii* has 150-167. Saharan horned vipers have a proportionately larger head and generally more upright horns. *C. cerastes* has a pair of enlarged tubercles between the eyes.

Distribution

Cerates cerastes hoofieni is known from south-western Saudi Arabia and Yemen. The full extent of its range is not known. The nominate form *C.c. cerastes* is known throughout North Africa, south to the Sahel complex. Also entering Sinai and possibly further east.

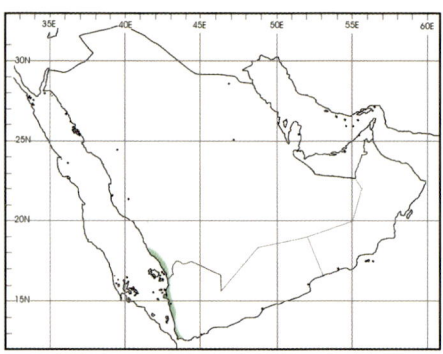

Natural History

Little is known of the Arabian subspecies of *Cerastes cerastes*. The nominate form is apparently more adaptable in its habitat requirements and avoids sand desert with sparse vegetation. They are found in sandy patches from scrubland to low-altitude rocky barrens and foothills. They are ambush predators relying on camouflage and a fast strike speed to catch prey. They are, however, very active at night and will cover long distances in search of suitable hunting ground. If encountered at night, horned vipers put on an impressive display, making a loud rasping sound

by rubbing lateral dorsal scales together while winding around in a roughly horseshoe formation, striking out. By day they are very tolerant of thoroughfare and appear quite torpid, unless their disturbance is prolonged.

Adults feed primarily on lizards and desert rodents. Babies feed predominantly on small geckos.

Top: *A captive specimen of the nominate form,* Cerastes cerastes cerastes *from unknown locality (North Africa).*

Above: Cerastes cf. cerastes hoofieni *from Al Khubah Market on the Yemen–Saudi Arabian border (Capture locality unknown).*

Arabian Horned Viper

Cerastes gasperettii   *Leviton & Anderson, 1984*

 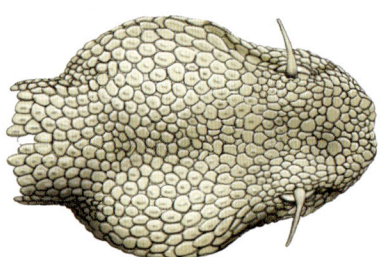

Description

Horned vipers may exceptionally reach 84 cm, but more commonly measure around 45-50 cm.

The head is flat, wide and roughly triangular in shape and is covered in fragmented, keeled scales. There may or may not be a horn above each eye. The pupils are elliptical, contracting into a slit in bright light. The neck is thin.

The body is stocky and robust in form. In well-fed specimens, the body is roundish in section. Lean individuals tend to be slightly compressed laterally. The tail is distinct, especially in females, as it becomes abruptly thinner behind the anal opening. Scales are heavily keeled, giving the snake a very rough appearance. The tail is between 10 and 15% of the total length (longer and thicker in males).

The colour and patterns of horned vipers varies regionally. Most commonly they are biscuit, tan or pale grey-brown, generally matching the sand on which they live. A single row of darker, wide transverse rectangles runs down the back. Towards the front and rear of the snake, these markings may break up to form a checkerboard appearance. A single row of spots runs along either flank. The tail may be sulphur-yellow, black or merely a continuation of the body colouration. The eye colour tends to match the general body colour. The ventral surface is white, cream or salmon.

Details

Mid-body scale rows: 27-35, heavily keeled
Anal: Entire, rarely divided
Subcaudals: 30-36, divided
Ventrals: 146-172, slightly keeled laterally
Head scales: Small fragmented head scales; 15-21 inter-orbital scales; 12-15 upper labials; 14 lower labials with 3 touching chin shields

Diagnostic Features

- Long outward-facing horn-like protrusion above the eye, or a slightly raised brow
- 15-21 inter-orbital scales
- Medium sized sandy-coloured viper that partially buries itself in the sand

Possible Confusion

The false horned viper, *Pseudocerastes fieldi* occurs in close proximity to *Cerastes gasperettii* in northern Saudi Arabia and Jordan. False horned vipers have a blunt, raised and rounded tubercle consisting of several scales, whereas horned specimens of *Cerastes gasperettii* have a single sharp spine. Hornless individuals have only a slightly raised brow-ridge.

Generally, their habitat choice is different, with Arabian horned vipers choosing a sand substrate over rock, or hard earth, which is where false horned vipers may be found.

A subspecies of the Sahara horned viper, *Cerastes cerastes hoofieni* is sympatric with Gasperetti's horned viper in parts of southern Saudi Arabia and Yemen. *C. cerastes* has 129-137 ventral scales, whereas *C. gasperettii* has 150-167. Arabian horned vipers lack the pair of tubercles on the head of the Saharan horned viper. Horned specimens tend to have horns that face outward, rather than the upright ones of *C. cerastes*.

Distribution

Throughout the Arabian Peninsula in suitable habitat. Absent from mountainous regions and the central Rub al-Khali, although they do penetrate quite far into the sands.

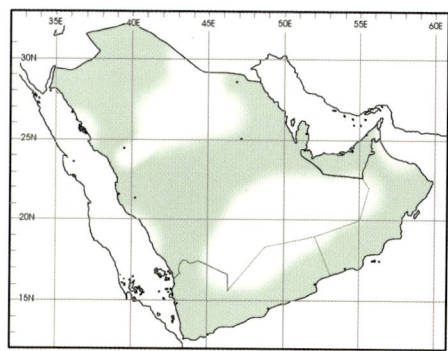

Natural History

They occupy sandy desert. Although they are more common in well-vegetated desert, they are found in most sandy environs.

Horned vipers feed on most small vertebrates. Adults would mostly feed on small rodents such as gerbils. Young vipers will eat lizards such as ground geckos (*Stenodactylus, Bunopis*).

Nocturnal, horned vipers are ambush predators usually lying partially buried in the sand with just the top of the head protruding. From this position, they ambush prey. They will only attempt escape if they are found out in the open; otherwise they tend to remain very still, and are very tolerant of thoroughfare at close quarters. Horned vipers cover huge distances at night and often lie in ambush in several spots in one night.

If threatened, they will coil up into a horseshoe-shape and rub the rough body scales together to create a loud rasping sound.

Oviparous, between 4 and 20 large oblong eggs are laid deep inside rodent burrows in the spring and early summer. The incubation period is from 70 to 80 days. Hatchlings are about 14 cm long, with a proportionately slender body and large head.

Although rare, the bite of this snake can produce life-threatening symptoms.

Symptoms may include: immediate local pain and swelling; discolouration of the bitten area and localized haemorrhaging; nausea and vomiting and occasional systemic haemorrhaging. Necrosis may set in around the bite site.

Top: *A hornless Arabian horned viper (Sharjah, UAE).*

Above: *A horned Arabian horned viper (Ajman, UAE).*

North East African Carpet Viper Complex

Including:
North East African Carpet Viper
Echis pyramidum pyramidum   (Geofry, St Hillaire, 1827)
Khosatzki's Saw-scaled Viper
Echis khosatzkii   Cherlin, 1990

Occurrence of *E. pyramidum* in Arabia

This complex represents at least two species of snakes from southern Arabia. *E. khosatzkii* was originally thought to be of the *E. carinatus* complex. Later it was thought to be a colour variant of *E. pyramidum* (which still holds in most current literature). Personal communications with researchers (Wüster, 2007) have revealed that this snake is genetically distinct from *Echis pyramidum*. Further work will be needed in western Yemen to determine the status of the remainder of this complex. In all likelihood, more species or subspecies will be revealed.

Echis pyramidum

Echis khosatzkii

Description

North East African carpet vipers may exceptionally reach over 60 cm, but the average adult length (Arabia) is around 45 cm. The head is slightly flattened, pear-shaped and covered in small imbricate scales. The eyes are large, pale gold to reddish and have elliptical, cat-like pupils. The head is distinct from the body although the neck is quite stout. The body is moderately thick and very slightly triangular in section. The dorsal scales are keeled and very rough. The tail is distinct in both sexes (longer and thicker in males) and constitutes about 9–13% of the total length.

The colour and pattern of this snake is variable. Most commonly, the background colour is sandy brown or greyish. A series of pale spots, blocks, or transverse oblong shapes, interspaced by dark brown or grey runs along the spine. Downward-pointing white crescents adorn either flank below each vertebral blotch.

Species Identification Guide

The points of these may meet, forming a prominent zigzag. The area surrounding the crescents and blotches is dark. A trident or clover pattern may or may not be present on the head. *Echis khosatzkii* from Dhofar may be virtually patternless, with only faint vertebral blotching. Usually the dorsal region has a wide row of dark-edged oscillations along the spine. One specimen from Salalah had zebra-like dark transverse bands over the entire body. *E. khosatzkii* is usually various shades of reddish brown.

Details

Mid-body scale rows: 25-33, keeled
Anal: Entire
Subcaudals: 29-48, entire
Ventrals: 155-189
Head scales: 10 upper labials; 11 lower labials; genial scales (medial margin of gular region) large and regularly arranged; 1 or 2 scale rows between eye and upper labial

Diagnostic Features

- Evenly placed large genial scales on throat
- Dorsal count can be less than 29 and a minimum of 25

Possible Confusion

Burton's carpet viper, *Echis coloratus* are similar and sympatric. Burton's carpet vipers are more slender with a proportionately thinner neck and larger, more bulbous head. *Echis carinatus* look very similar to some colour morphs, but have genial scales arranged in irregular rows and tend to inhabit sand desert. It is unclear if the two are sympatric. The Khosatzki's saw-scaled viper differs from typical *E. pyramidum* in having a fairly broad head as an adult. They also differ in patterning, with *E. khosatzkii* having oscillations or indistinct blotches with an overall reddish colour, compared to *E. pyramidum* that is usually brown or grey with rhombs or blocks on the back and a prominent white zigzag on the flanks.

Distribution

Throughout North East Africa from northern Kenya; Ethiopia; Somalia; Sudan; Eritrea and Egypt. In Arabia they are found in south-western Saudi Arabia from about 18°N, south to Aden, then east along the Hadramaut. *Echis khosatzkii* represents the complex in Dhofar, as far east as about 57°E.

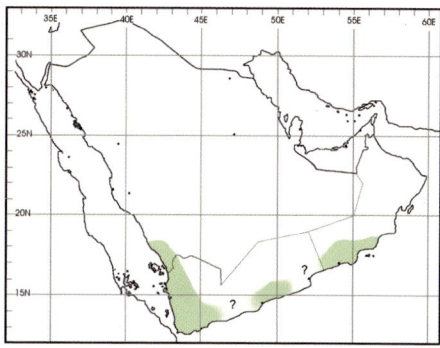

Natural History

They normally occupy well-vegetated areas, from mountain grassland, vegetated deserts, coastal plains and wadis. This species is well known from gardens and other human structures.

Opportunistic, *Echis pyramidum* eats a wide range of vertebrates and invertebrates. Adults most commonly feed on geckos, but will eat rodents, amphibians, birds and soft-bodied invertebrates including scorpions.

North East African saw-scaled vipers are nocturnal. In Africa, they could be held accountable for much human casualty each year. Bites appear to be rarer in Arabia, although this snake is greatly feared, particularly in the Yemen Tihama.

If threatened, they become irascible and will coil up into a horseshoe-shape rubbing laterally opposing scales together to create a rasping sound. They will also strike out violently with full intention of biting!

Ovoviviparous, the young are born in late spring or early summer. Large females produce clutches of 10 babies or more.

Echis khosatzkii seems to be unique in that it does not employ a side-winding mode of locomotion.

Echis khosatzkii *(Khor Rouri, Dhofar).*

Above: A North East African carpet viper from Ghedaref, Sudan.

Below: A Khosatzkii's viper from Salalah, Dhofar.

Sindh Saw-scaled Viper

Echis carinatus sochureki   *Stemmler, 1969*

Description

Saw-scaled vipers reach a maximum length of around 70 cm, but are more commonly around 35-45 cm in total length. The head is slightly flattened and pear-shaped. The eyes are large with elliptical, cat-like pupils and bright reddish-brown irises. The neck is thin, and the head distinct from the body. The body is fairly thick and very slightly flattened in section. The tail is distinct and constitutes about 8-13% of the total length (longer and thicker in males).

Colour and pattern are variable. Most commonly, the base colour is brown, grey or tan, with a prominent series of white blocks or blotches along the spine. These markings are surrounded by dark brown or grey, which fades outwardly. In some specimens the markings split and alternate on either side of the spine. A row of small, whitish, downward-pointing crescents runs along the flanks.

The ventral surface is usually white, with pale brown or grey blocks or speckles towards the centre of each scale.

Details

Mid-body scale rows: 25-33, keeled
Ventrals: 155-189
Anal: Entire
Subcaudals: 29-48, entire
Head scales: 14-20 circum-orbital scales; 2 or 3 series of scales between the eye and the labial; 10-12 upper labials; 3-4 lower labials in contact with chin shields; head shields replaced by small imbricate scales

Species Identification Guide

Diagnostic Features

- Only saw-scaled viper in sand deserts of eastern Arabia
- Genial scales large and regular
- Mid-dorsal scales humped slightly

Possible Confusion

Sindh saw-scaled vipers differ from Oman carpet viper, *Echis omanensis* and Khosatzki's saw-scaled viper, *Echis khosatzkii* in the structure of the genial scales, which in this species are large and regularly arranged. Oman carpet vipers have a thinner, more compressed body and head that expands from behind the eye, and is almost never found in sandy desert.

Distribution

In suitable habitat throughout the Eastern Province of Saudi Arabia, Qatar, United Arab Emirates north-eastern Oman, south, to just north-east of Dhofar. Also Masirah island. Elsewhere they are known from Pakistan and coastal Iran.

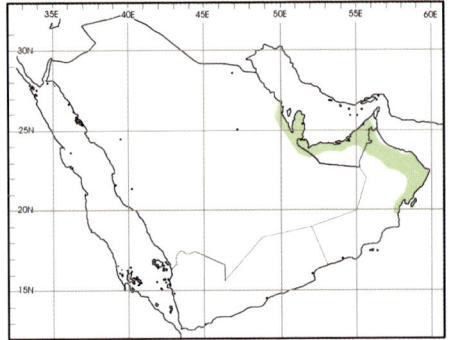

Natural History

They are most commonly found in vegetated sandy desert, gravel plain and arid grassland. Found up to 500 m above sea level, but generally at much lower altitudes. Frequently found in agricultural and urbanized areas.

Babies feed primarily on geckos and soft-bodied insects such as crickets. Adults feed on any small vertebrates, including rodents, shrews, lizards and fledgling birds. They also feed on scorpions and other invertebrates.

Saw-scaled vipers are common within their range. They are often found in gardens etc and seem to thrive near humans, no doubt taking advantage of the presence of rodents and house geckos. They are nocturnal and, as with horned vipers, travel large distances each night. Prey is ambushed from the shelter of a stone, shrub etc. Saw-scaled vipers do not shuffle into the sand as horned vipers do.

If disturbed they will lapse into a horseshoe-shape and rub laterally opposing scales against each other to produce an impressive rasping sound. They are reluctant to bite and are tolerant of passive thoroughfare. The strike, however, is fast and accurate.

Breeding takes place in early summer between 5 and 11 fully formed babies are born, usually down a moist burrow. Here they will remain for a few days until they shed their skin and move away.

Above: *A pale Sindh saw-scaled viper from Al Ain, UAE.*

Below: *A typical specimen from Sharjah, UAE.*

Burton's Carpet Viper

Echis coloratus   Gunther, 1878

Description

Carpet vipers may reach a maximum total length of around 75 cm, but adults average about 50-60 cm. The head is large, bulbous and pear-shaped and is covered in small fragmented, keeled scales. Eyes are moderately large and usually pale, with elliptical, cat-like pupils. The neck is thin. The body is moderately thick, and slightly laterally compressed. *E. coloratus* is generally more slender than other Arabian *Echis* species. The tail is distinct in females, being shorter and narrow. In males there is a slight hemipenal bulge. The tail constitutes between 10 and 13 % of the total body length. The body scales are keeled, and appear velvety.

The base colour is grey, tan, pinkish or brown. A series of dark-edged pale dorsal spots or squares runs the length of the body. These markings may run evenly down the spine, or alternate on either side forming a rough zigzag. The spaces in between the spots, on the vertebral line, are darker than the flanks. The flanks are barred in sympathy to the dorsal patterning. There may or may not be a faint trident-shape on the top of the head. The underside is white or light grey.

Note: See full-body illustrations of *Echis omanensis* for more colour variations of *E. coloratus*.

Details

Mid-body scale-rows: 31-35, keeled
Ventrals: 174-205
Anal: Entire
Subcaudals: 42-52 (entire)
Head scales: Fragmented, keeled; no supra-ocular shield; 12-15 upper labials; 3-4 series of scales between eye and labials

Diagnostic Features

- Head bulges behind the eyes in a pear-shape
- 3-4 scale rows between eye and upper labial

Possible Confusion

North East African carpet vipers, *Echis pyramidum* and Khosatzki's saw-scaled viper, *Echis khosatzkii* superficially resemble this species. Burton's carpet vipers have a head that bulges out from behind the eyes significantly. The other two species have rounder heads with no visible break in the outline at the eye region.

Distribution

From eastern Egypt through Sinai, Palestine and Jordan to north-western Saudi Arabia along the west coast and parts of the central interior (near Riyadh and west) to Aden and the Hadramaut. There is an isolated population in Dhofar.

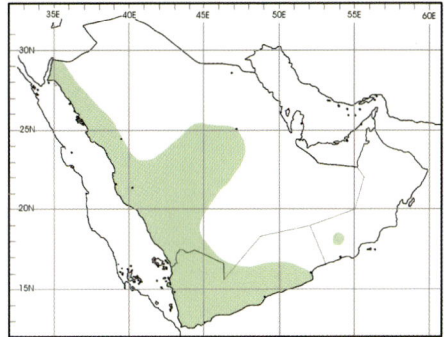

Natural History

Opportunistic, carpet vipers feed on rodents, lizards, birds and toads.

   Nocturnal, they become active shortly after sunset and start to forage, stopping at several points to lie in wait for prey. During the day, they can often be seen resting next to pools in the shade. They become quite resident in an area, and have regular basking spots. If disturbed, they will strike out with minimal provocation and create a loud rasping sound by rubbing laterally opposing scales together.

   They are oviparous, laying 4-10 eggs deep in fissures or down rodent burrows in the spring or early summer.

Above & below: Specimens of the Burton's carpet viper from Jordan.

Oman Carpet Viper

Echis omanensis   *Babocsay, 2004*

Description

This species is virtually identical in appearance to the Burton's carpet viper, *Echis coloratus*. Oman carpet vipers may reach a maximum of 75-80 cm in total length, but adults average 45-50 cm. The head is large, bulbous and roughly pear-shaped. The head is covered in small keeled scales with a velvety appearance. The eyes are moderately large with elliptical pupils. The iris colour is variable, but usually paler than the base colour. Some specimens have dark blackish-grey irises. The neck region is very thin and the body is moderately stout and slightly compressed, being covered in small keeled scales. The tail is distinct, particularly in females and constitutes around 15-17% of the total length.

In colour, Oman carpet vipers are extremely variable, whereas the pattern remains more or less consistent. The base colour is most commonly tan, greyish or pinkish, with a series of dark edged pale dorsal spots, blocks or rhombs running along the back. These may or may not break up to alternate in a checkerboard or zigzag pattern. The flanks are barred or have a series of spots matching the dorsal pattern. The head may or may not have an X-shape or a trident marking on it. The ventral surface may be grey, white or pinkish.

Note: See full-body illustrations of *Echis coloratus* for more colour variations of *E. omanensis*.

Details

Mid-body scale rows: 31-35, keeled
Anal: Entire
Subcaudals: 49-58, entire
Ventrals: 184-194
Head scales: Fragmented, keeled; no supraocular; 12-14 upper labials; lower prenasal often missing; upper prenasal often fused with nasal; subnasal often missing or fused with nasal; gular scales preceding preventrals are round or slightly elongate; preventrals round or slightly elongate

Species Identification Guide

Diagnostic Features

- Bulbous head that expands behind the eyes
- Irascible small viper that rubs its scales together in defense and lives in rocky habitat

Possible Confusion

Oman carpet vipers may share part of their range with Sindh saw-scaled vipers, *Echis carinatus sochureki*. Normally the Sindh saw-scaled vipers inhabit sandy deserts and gravel plains west of the Oman Mountains, but they follow green belts well outside of their natural range. Oman carpet vipers have very bulbous heads and thinner neck regions than Sindh saw-scaled vipers. They are also more slender and slightly smoother in appearance.

Distribution

The eastern mountain complex of Oman and United Arab Emirates.

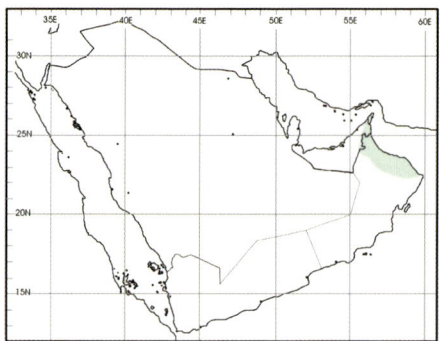

Natural History

Oman carpet vipers live in mountain valleys and surrounding rocky terrain. They are seldom found above 800 m altitude. They are common in wadis containing permanent water, where they often become resident at pools.

Their diet consists of geckos, rodents, birds, toads and fish.

Oman carpet vipers are nocturnal, becoming active in the late afternoon and early evening to forage between rocks and down holes. They also regularly ambush prey from strategic points. Although nocturnal, these snakes are often observed resting during the day, particularly in winter. If disturbed during the day they are generally quite torpid and lethargic at first, becoming aggressive if provoked. By night they are highly aggressive and will not hesitate to bite.

Carpet vipers are capable of causing human fatality although this could be considered exceptional. Antivenom is effective against the bite.

Above & below: *Two colour morphs of the Oman carpet viper from Fujairah, UAE.*

Persian Horned Viper

Pseudocerastes persicus persicus

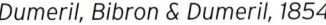

Dumeril, Bibron & Dumeril, 1854

Description

Persian horned vipers reach a maximum size of around 86 cm but are more commonly between 50 and 60 cm in total length. The head is wide and sub-triangular if viewed from above, and is distinct with a thinner neck region. A blunt horn-like projection, consisting of several scales sits above each eye. The eyes are moderate with pale irises and elliptical pupils. The body is thick and slightly flattened in section. The tail is only distinct in females and constitutes around 8-10% of the total length.

As with the Field's horned viper *Pseudocerastes fieldi*, Persian horned vipers occur in a variety of colour generally matching the substrate on which they live. Most commonly Oman Mountain specimens are greyish brown with alternating darker brown bars across the back and flanks with a whitish ventral surface. Chocolate-brown, patternless specimens are also not uncommon in the region.

Details

Mid-body scale rows: 23-24, keeled
Ventrals: 144-158
Anal: Entire
Subcaudals: 38-48, divided
Head scales: (*Those that differ from P. fieldi*) 13-23 circum-orbital scales; 1-2 or 1 and 2 supranasals

Diagnostic Features

- Medium sized horned viper from high altitude areas in the Oman Mountains
- Horns consist of several small scales forming blunt protrusion
- 144-158 ventrals

Possible Confusion

Unlikely to be confused with other snakes in its range. Oman carpet vipers live in the same mountains but lack any horns above the eyes.

Distribution

This species seems to be distributed throughout the eastern mountains of Oman and UAE at altitudes above 600 m. Most common in Jebel Akhdar and the higher points of the Musandam Peninsula. Elsewhere they are known from Iran, Pakistan and Afghanistan.

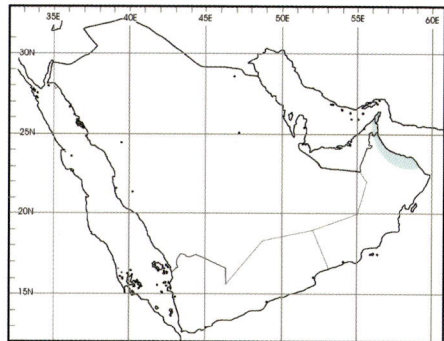

Natural History

A rarely encountered species, the Persian horned viper lives on exposed mountain tops and plateaus. The young probably feed on geckos and small Agamids (*Pseudotrapelis* etc). Adults feed on rodents, Agamid lizards and birds. The possible reason that they only inhabit high altitude regions in Arabia, is because they are out-competed by the more common Oman carpet vipers in the valley floors. As an Asian remnant, they also probably require slightly lower temperatures than the carpet vipers. In Asia, they are found at a variety of altitudes. Although nocturnal, Persian horned vipers have mostly been observed sunning themselves on rocks in the mid-morning. These diurnal sightings tend to increase during the winter months.

One of the many colour morphs, Pseudocerastes persicus *from the Oman Mountains.*

Field's Horned Viper

Pseudocerastes fieldi   *Schmidt, 1930*

Description

Field's horned vipers reach a maximum size of around 90 cm, but are more commonly between 50 and 60 cm in total length. The head is wide and flattened with a prominent horn-like protrusion above each eye, consisting of several small scales. The head is distinct from the body with a thin neck area. The body is stout and slightly flattened in section. The tail is distinct in females but not in males and constitutes around 10-12% of the total length.

The colour is highly variable and normally matches the substrate on which the snake lives. Base colours of grey, tan, brown or blackish have all been recorded. Some are without dorsal patterns, but most have darker, alternating rows of blocks or bars on the back, with similar, smaller blocks or spots mirroring them on the flanks.

Details

Mid-body scale rows: 21-23, keeled except the outer rows which may be feebly keeled or smooth
Ventrals: 134-138
Anal: Entire
Subcaudals: 41-48, divided
Head scales: Small imbricate, keeled scales covering head; blunt horn above each eye consisting of a cluster of scales; 2 scales between nasal and rostral; 3 series of scales between eye and labial; 14-18 circum-orbital scales; 1-2 supranasals; 13 upper labials; 4 lower labials in contact with anterior chin shields

Species Identification Guide

Diagnostic Features

- Stout viper with blunt horns comprised of many small scales
- Dorsal scales are keeled except for the outer rows

Possible Confusion

Arabian horned vipers, *Cerastes gasperettii* are superficially similar but have horns consisting of a single sharp scale each, as opposed to a blunt cluster of scales of the Field's horned viper. Hornless Arabian horned vipers have only a slightly raised brow-ridge.

Distribution

From Sinai, across the northern Middle East to northern Iraq and Iran. This species just enters northern Saudi Arabia.

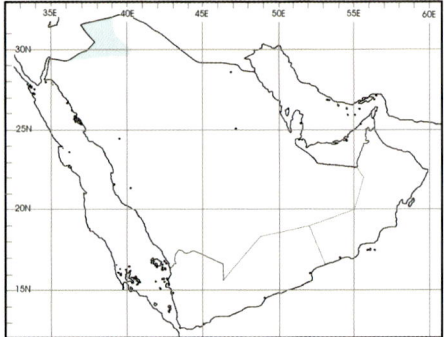

Natural History

These snakes prefer firm substrates and are absent from sand deserts. They are most commonly associated with rocky terrain rich in cover, with or without vegetation. They are found at most altitudes up to around 1,000 m. Young Field's vipers feed on geckos and other small lizards, whereas adults feed primarily on rodents, as well as larger Lacertid and Agamid lizards and small birds. Unlike many other desert vipers, Field's horned vipers do not side-wind, but employ a rectilinear type of locomotion if undisturbed, or a more serpentine style if disturbed.

They are oviparous, laying up to 21 eggs in midsummer. The embryos are already well developed on parturition, and the eggs only take about a month to hatch.

Above & below: *A dark Field's horned viper from Jordan. This specimen was living on dark coloured volcanic rock.*

Levantine Viper, Blunt-nosed Viper

Macrovipera lebetina   *(Linnaeus, 1758)*

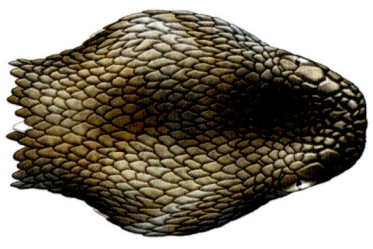

Description

Levantine vipers may exceptionally reach 1.3 m in total length, but adults average 70-80 cm. The head is wide, triangular and covered in small keeled scales. The neck region is thin. The eyes are moderately small with pale irises and elliptical pupils. The body is thick and long, being slightly compressed in section (although the body can be flattened at will), and is covered in small keeled scales. The tail is distinct, particularly in females and constitutes 10-13% of the total length.

Levantine vipers are variable in colour and pattern. Most commonly the base colour is sandy brown, tan, pinkish or light grey with darker brown or grey rhomboid bars along the back. These may be entire or broken into a near-continuous zigzag, or a checkerboard pattern. A row of blotches or blocks runs along either flank, alternating with the dorsal patterns. Some specimens have an overall mottled appearance with only the slightest suggestion of the aforementioned pattern. Other specimens have thinner, wider saddles, closer resembling banding. Normally a faint stripe runs from the eye to the angle of the jaw. A second stripe runs from the eye down to the lip.

Details

Mid-body scale rows: 23-27, strongly keeled
Anal: Entire
Subcaudals: 33-58, divided
Ventrals: 126-181, well developed
Head scales: Diameter of eye less than the distance from lip; rostral as deep as broad and nearly reaching upper surface of snout and in contact with 2 or 3 apical scales; upper head scales subimbricate, keeled, occasionally smooth on forehead and snout region; 7-12 longitudinal inter-orbital scales; 12-18 circum-orbital scales; 2 or 3 series of scales between eye and labials; keeled temporal scales, concave nasal with centrally placed nostril; 9-12 upper labials; 4 or 5 lower labials in contact with chin shields

Diagnostic Features

- Large, stout, long viper with slender neck
- Angular head, slightly raised eyes, raised brow-ridges

Possible Confusion

Levantine vipers are superficially similar to many other Arabian vipers. Carpet vipers and hornless specimens of the horned viper may look similar. In the case of the horned viper, they are proportionately much shorter and fatter than levantine vipers, the head is flatter and wider, and the dorsal scales are extremely rough. Horned vipers and carpet vipers rub scales together to create a warning sound. Levantine vipers do not. Saw-scaled vipers may resemble young specimens of the levantine viper. Levantine vipers have a raised brow-ridge, slightly elevated eyes, and a wider, more angular head, with a blunt, flat snout.

Distribution

From eastern Europe, through western Asia, the northern regions of the Middle East to the Mediterranean. A single specimen was recorded from Yemen in 1932.

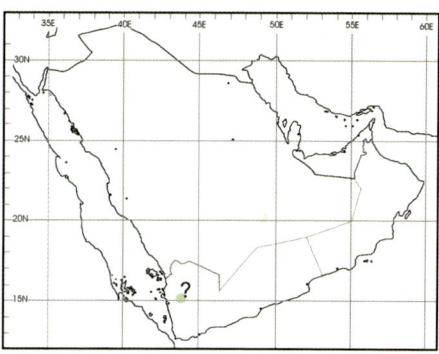

Natural History

Levantine vipers inhabit a range of habitats usually rich in vegetation and cover, from Mediterranean scrub to semi-arid mountains and foothills. They are common in agricultural areas

and plantations. The young feed mostly on geckos and other lizards, whereas adults consume mostly warm-blooded prey such as rodents and birds.

Sluggish during the day, this snake is reluctant to bite. They are irascible at night however and hiss loudly if antagonized, often with very little provocation. Some authors believe this species to be ovoviviparous, while others have recorded that northern populations are ovoviviparous and southern populations are oviparous.

This species constitutes a significant risk to agricultural workers and others in the field and has caused human fatality in areas outside the range covered by this book.

Above & top: *Two colour morphs of the levantine viper from Jordan.*

A Word on Sharjah's Involvement in Arabian Conservation

Arid environments are among the most fragile on earth. They maintain a very precarious balance in order to ensure the survival of species within the greater ecosystem, and have limited repairing function should humans interfere and upset this dynamic equilibrium. Since the discovery of oil in Arabia, development and urban sprawl have consumed, or otherwise damaged huge tracts of wilderness at an unprecedented rate. Add hunting to this problem and the result is that some species, such as the Arabian cheetah and Arabian ostrich have been rendered completely extinct. Others, such as Arabian leopards and Arabian tahr are teetering on the threshold of extinction, quite literally depending on a handful of motivated people, often working against the material interests of those who make decisions, to take action for the future survival of these creatures.

Reptiles, and in particular snakes, have faired better than most vertebrates due to their resilient and adaptable nature, but that is not to say that they are immune from extinction. Direct persecution takes its toll on snakes each year, but these numbers are negligible when one considers how many acres of habitat are being developed each day in the region. Cement-walled highways create barriers through which animals cannot pass, thus fragmenting the existing patches of habitat even further. Highways often result in peripheral development including industrial areas, residential areas and all the associated roads, dump sites and other 'side effects'. With much of the region possessing poor urban planning strategy, the problem of urban creep will just increase.

At a time where parts of the region are responsible for consuming more of the earth's resources per person, than any other on the planet, the future of desert ecology throughout much of Arabia looks very bleak indeed.

Despite this very dismal outlook, there is much of the Arabian Peninsula that remains relatively intact, particularly in the central areas and further south. For the rest, several initiatives have been formed to address these problems and take action before it's too late.

BREEDING CENTRE FOR ENDANGERED ARABIAN WILDLIFE

The Breeding Centre for Endangered Arabian Wildlife was opened in 1997 by the Environment and Protected Areas Authority of Sharjah, under the patronage of His Highness Dr Sheikh Sultan Bin Mohammed Al Qassimi.

The primary objective of the centre is to maintain and reproduce breeding species of terrestrial fauna indigenous to the Arabian Peninsula with priorities given to endangered species. Additionally, qualified staff from the Centre were detailed to conduct research on various species in the wild and use these findings to further increase our knowledge of Arabian fauna. Over the years, the Breeding Centre has grown to the point where it houses the single most important collection of endangered Middle Eastern wildlife, from frogs and fish, to leopards and oryx. This collection could be regarded as a live gene bank representing those animals facing possible extinction in the wild.

ARABIA'S WILDLIFE CENTRE

In 1999 Arabia's Wildlife Centre was opened adjacent to the Breeding Centre. This is the first visitor's centre completely dedicated to species indigenous to the Arabian Peninsula. Arabia's Wildlife Centre fulfills another vitally important aspect of conservation, namely education. Thousands of school children and other members of the public visit this modern facility annually and learn about the plight of Arabian wildlife.

CONSERVATION MEETINGS

Identifying a need for cooperation with other Arab countries, and addressing greater ecological issues facing Arabia, the Breeding Centre hosted the first regional conservation workshop in 2000. Since then the workshops have become an annual event with delegates coming from all over the Peninsula and abroad to add their own expertise and discuss problems, concerns and strategy. The content of the workshop started off with key species such as Arabian leopards while the process was still in its teething stage, but later expanded to cover all species from invertebrates up. The workshop has now gone to the next level in 2007, by focusing discussion on protected areas for the entire region.

Selected References

AL MOHANNA, S Y & MEAKINS, R H: 1997. First record of Melanistic Whip snake *Coluber jugularis*, Linnaeus, 1758, from the Arabian Peninsula. *Zoology in the Middle East.* Vol. 14:73

AL MOHANNA, S Y & AMR, Z S. First Record of the Mole Viper *Atractaspis engaddensis* in Jordan. *Zoology in the Middle East.* Vol. 11:47

AMR, Z S & AMR, S S: 1983. Snakebite in Jordan. *The Snake.* Vol. 15:81-85

ARNOLD, A E: 1982. Reptiles of Saudi Arabia – A New Species of Semaphore Gecko and a New Dwarf Snake from Southwestern Arabia. *Fauna of Saudi Arabia.* Vol. 4

ARNOLD, E N & GALLAGHER, M D: 1975. Reptiles and Amphibians from the Mountains of Northern Oman. *Journal of Oman Studies special report, Oman flora & fauna survey*

ARNOLD, E N: 1980. Reptiles and Amphibians of Dhofar, Southern Arabia. *Journal of Oman Studies special report.* Vol. 2:273-332

ARNOLD, E N: 1982. Reptiles of Saudi Arabia. A New Species of Semaphore gecko (Pristurus: Gekkonidae) and a New Dwarf Snake (Eirenis: Colubridae) from Southwestern Arabia. *Fauna of Saudi Arabia.* Vol. 4:68-477

BABOCSAY, G: 2003. Geographic Variation in *Echis Coloratus* (Viperdae: Ophidia) in the Levant with the Description of a New Subspecies. *Zoology in the Middle East.* Vol. 41: 9-11

BABOCSAY, G: 2004. A New Species of Saw-Scaled Viper of the *Echis Coloratus* Complex (Ophidia: Viperidae) from Oman, Eastern Arabia. *Systematics and Biodiversity.* Vol. 1 (4): 503-514

BAHA EL DIN, S M: 1992. Notes on the Herpetology of North Sinai. *British Herpetological Society Bulletin.* Vol. 41: 9-11

BAHA EL DIN, S M: 2006. A Guide to the Reptiles and Amphibians of Egypt. *American University in Cairo Press*

BDOLAH, A: 1986. Comparison of venom from two subspecies of the false horned viper (*Pseudocerastes persicus*). Toxicon 24: 867-875

BOSTANCHI, H, S C ANDERSON, H G KAMI & T J PAPENFUS: 2006. A new species of *Pseudocerastes* with elaborate tail ornamentation from western Iran (Squamata: Viperidae). Proceedings of the California Academy of Sciences. Vol. 57: 443–450

CHERLIN, V A: 1990. Taxonomic of the genus Echis (Viperidae). II. An analysis of taxonomy and description of new forms. *Proc. Zool. Inst. USSR Academy of Science. Leningrad.* Vol. 207: 193-223

CHERLIN, V A & BORKIN, L J: 1990. Taxonimic of the snakes of the genus *Echis* (Viperidae). I. An analysis of taxonomy and descriptions of new forms. *Proc. Zool. Inst. USSR Academy of Science. Leningrad.* Vol. 207: 175-192

CORKILL, N L & COCHRANE, J A: 1966. The Snakes of the Arabian Peninsula and Sokotra. *Journal of the Bombay Natural History Society.* Vol. 62: 475-506

CUNNINGHAM, P L: 2002. Review of the false horned viper (Dumeril, Bibron & Dumeril, 1854). From the UAE and Northern Oman. *Tribulus.* Vol. 12.1

CUNNINGHAM, P L: 1998. Snake Bite – A case report from the UAE. *Tribulus.* Vol. 8.2

Selected References

CUNNINGHAM, P L & HANDLY, D L: 2000 *Psammophis schokari schokari* (Forskal, 1775) An arborial hunter. *Tribulus*. Vol. 10.2

DEAN, B: 1938. Note on the Sea Snake *Pelamis plaurus* (Linnaeus). *Science*. Vol. 88:144-145

DISI, A M: 2002. Herpetofauna of Jordan. Jordan Country study on biological diversity

DUNSON, W A & DUNSON, M K: 1973. Convergient Evolution of sublingual salt glands in the Marine File Snake and the True Sea Snakes. *Journal of Comp. Physiology*. Vol. 86:193-208

GASPERETTI, J: 1988. Snakes of Arabia. *Fauna of Saudi Arabia*. Vol. 9:169-450

FITZSIMONS, F W: 1919. Snakes of South Africa. *T Maskew Miller*. Cape Town, SA

FITZSIMONS, F W: 1962. Snakes of Southern Africa. *Purnell and Sons*

GASPERETTI, J: 1972. A Preliminary Sketch of the Snakes of the Arabian Peninsula. *Journal of the Saudi Arabian Natural History Society*. Vol. 12: 1-72

GASPERETTI, J: 1976. A Very Rare Snake - *Coluber elegantissimus*. *Journal of the Saudi Arabian Natural History Society*. Vol. 18: 13-15

GASPERETTI, J: 1977. Snakes in Arabia. *Journal of the Saudi Arabian Natural History Society*. Vol. 19: 3-16

ISMAEL, M & MEMISH, Z A: 2003. Venomous snakes of Saudi Arabia and the Middle East: A Keynote for Travelers. *International Journal of Antimicrobial Agents*. Vol. 21: 164-169

KEELE, C A: 1963. Venoms and the Causes of Pain. *New Scientist*. Vol. 17:396-399

KURNIK, D, HAVIV, Y & VOCHVA, E: 1999. A Snakebite by the Burrowing Asp *Atractaspis engaddensis*. *Toxicon*. Vol. 37: 223 – 227

LENK, P, H W HERRMANN, U JOGER, & M WINK: 1999. Phylogeny and taxonomic subdivision of *Bitis* (Reptilia: Viperidae) based on molecular evidence. *Kaupia*. Vol. 8: 31-38

LEVITON, A E: 1986. Description of a New Species of *Coluber* (Reptilia: Serpentes: Colubridae) from the Southern Tihama of Saudi Arabia, with Comments on the Biogeography of Southwestern Arabia. *Fauna of Saudi Arabia*. Vol. 8 436-446

LEVITON, A E, ANDERSON, S C, ADLER, K & MINTON, S A: 1992. Handbook to the middle East Amphibians and Reptiles. *Society for the Study of Amphibians and Reptiles*

NADY, Z T, JOGER, U, WINK, M, GLAW, F & VENCES, M: 2003. Multiple Colonization of Madagascar and Socotra by Colubrid Snakes: Evidence from Nuclear and Mitochondrial Gene Phylogenies. *Royal Society, London B. 2003*

SCHÄTTE, B & GASPERETTI, J A: Contribution to the Herpetofauna of Southwestern Arabia. *Fauna of Saudi Arabia*. Vol: 14

SCHÄTTE, B & DESVOIGNES, A: 1999. The Herpetofauna of Southern Yemen and the Sokotra archipelago. *Museum d' Histoire Naturelle, Geneve*

SCHLEICH, H H, KASTLE, W & KABISCH, K: 1996. Amphibians and Reptiles of North Africa. *Koeltx Scientific Books*

Selected References

SCHMIDT, K P: 1953. Amphibians and Reptiles of Yemen. *Fieldiana*. Vol. 34:253-261

SCHNEEMANN, M, CATHOMAS, R, LAIDLAW, S T, EL NAHAS, A M, THEAKSON, R D G, WARREL, D A: 2004. Life-Threatening Envenomation by the Saharan Horned Viper (*Cerastes cerastes*) Causing Micro Angiopathic Haelolysis, coagulopathy and Acute Renal Failure: Clinical Cases and Review. *Q. J. Med.* 97; 717-727

SIVAN, N & WERNER, Y L: 2003. Revision of the Middle Eastern Dwarf Snakes Commonly Assigned to *Eirenis coronella* (Colubridae). Zoology in the Middle East. Vol. 28: 39-59

SUTHERLAND, S K: 1976. Treatment of Snakebite in Australia and Papua New Guinea. *Australian Family Physician*. Vol: 5

TILBURY, C R: An Annoted Checklist of Some of the Commoner Reptiles Occuring Around Riyadh, Kingdom of Saudi Arabia. *Journal of the Herpetological Association of Africa*

VAN DER KOOIJ, J: 2001. The Herpetofauna of the Sultanate of Oman. Part 4: Terrestrial Snakes. *Podarcus*

WERNER, Y L: 1991. Notable Herpetofaunal Records from TransJordan. *Zoology in the Middle East*. Vol. 5: 37-41

WERNER, Y L: 1994. Head Size Variation in *Cerastes* (Ophidia: Viperidae) parallels in body size variation in potential prey. (Rodenta: Gerbillinae). *The snake*. Vol. 26: 57-60

WERNER, Y L & SIVAN, N: 1992. Systematics and Zoogeography of *Cerastes* (Ophibie: Viperidae) in the Levant: Taxonomy, Ecology and Zoogeography. *The Snake*. Vol. 24: 34-49

WERNER, Y L, SIVAN, N, KUSHIER, V & MOTRO, U: A Statistical approach to variations in *Cerastes* (Opdidia: Viperidae) With the Description of Two Endemic Subspecies. *Kaupia (Darmstadt)*. Vol. 8: 83-97

WERNER, Y L, VERDIER, A, ROSEMAN, & SIVAN, N: 1991. Systematics and Zoogeography of *Cerastes* (Ophidia: Viperidae) in the Levant: 1, Distinuishing Arabian from African 'Cerastes cerastes'. *The Snake*. Vol. 23: 90-100

WONG, A: 2000. Species Diversity and Ecological Distribution of Sea Snakes (Sub-family Hydrophiinae) on the West Coast of Sabah. *Thesus: University of Malaysia, Sarawak*

WÜSTER, W, GOLAY, P & WARRELL, D A: 1999. Synopsis of Recent Developments in Venomous Snake Systematics, *Ho 3. Toxicon*. Vol. 37: 1123-1129

Contact Details

BREEDING CENTRE FOR ENDANGERED ARABIAN WILDLIFE
PO Box 29922, Sharjah, UAE
Tel: (+971 6) 5311 212
Fax: (+971 6) 5311 156
e-mail: breeding@epaa-shj.gov.ae

ARABIA'S WILDLIFE CENTRE
Tel: (+971 6) 5311 999
Fax: (+971 6) 5311 419

ENVIRONMENT AND PROTECTED AREAS AUTHORITY (EPAA)
Tel: (+971 6) 5311 501
Fax: (+971 6) 5311 419
e-mail: epaa@emirates.net.ae

About the Author

Born in South Africa, Damien Egan started working professionally with reptiles in 1995. Since then he has held the position of curator of the Swadini Reptile Park, in Limpopo, South Africa, and curator of reptiles at the old Transvaal Snake Park in Gauteng, South Africa. For the last eight years he has been working at the Breeding Centre for Endangered Arabian Wildlife, first as an assistant, and later as the HoD of Herpetology and Freshwater Fishes. Here he supervises the maintenance and breeding of a large collection of Arabian reptiles, amphibians and freshwater fish. His work has taken him to some of the most remote parts of Arabia, doing surveys, and conducting talks on snakes and reptiles.

He has kept close company with all manner of reptiles, amphibians and other small wildlife from a tender age.

DAMIEN EGAN
e-mail: nkuku1001@gmail.com

Photographic Credits

Jonathan Ali Khan - 14T

William R Branch - 81, 180B

Damien Egan - Front cover, back cover, half-title, 6T, 7, 9, 10B, 11T, 11BL & BR, 12T & B, 13T, 13BL & BR, 14B, 15T, 15M, 16T, 16BL, 17T & B, 18T, 18BL & BR, 19T, 19M, 19B, 20T & B, 21, 22T & B, 23, 24TL, 24B, 25T & B, 26T & B, 28T & B, 29T & B, 32, 33TL & TR, 33M & B, 35B, 36, 42, 43, 44TL & TR, 44B, 45T & B, 46T & B, 47, 48, 49, 54, 55, 62T & B, 68T & B, 71T & B, 74T & B, 86T & B, 94T & B, 100M, 105T & M & B, 116T & B, 123T & B, 126T & B, 132, 133T & B, 136, 137T & B, 139T & B, 147T & B, 150B, 156T, 150BL & BR, 170T & B, 173T & B, 176T & B, 183T & B, 189T & B, 199, 200, 206

Drew Gardner - 57, 192

Wulf Haacke - 107, 113T & B

David Hegner - 65T & B

Koji Kawai (RSCN, Jordan) - 195T & B

David Modrý - 77, 88, 89T & B, 100T & B, 118, 140T & B, 186T, 198T

Peter Phelan - 15B, 16BR

Tanya Sadler - 35T

Paul Vercammen - 10T

Harold Voris - 24TR, 142, 144, 153, 159, 162, 167

Wolfgang Wüster - 52, 110T & B, 179, 180T, 186B, 198B

James A Pointdexter II (USGS) - 128, 129T & B

Transvaal Museum - 97

Fareed Krupp - 150T & M, 165T & B

T: top; B: bottom; L: left; R: right; M: middle.

Index to Common Names

Index to Scientific Names